What People
From Burned

"*From Burned Out to Fired Up* is a must-have book for every woman who feels burned out or just bored by her career or life. This is not just another career change book. Leslie Godwin shows you how to shed the habits, beliefs and stressors that cause burnout and shows you how to discover and achieve career goals that are truly important to you. *From Burned Out to Fired Up* gives you both the guiding light and the tools you need to climb out from under and put meaning back in your life."

—Janet Attard
founder, *BusinessKnowhow.com*
author, *The Home Office and Small Business Answer Book*

"Leslie Godwin has written a rich and resourceful guide for the woman who feels her life has run away with her. Women and their professional coaches and counselors will find valuable wisdom, role models and practical advice for revitalization and renewal."

—Joan Goldsmith
organizational consultant and author,
The Art of Waking People Up: Cultivating Awareness and Authenticity at Work

"Do you really feel truly happy? Are you truly satisfied with yourself, your career, your family or your life? If you answered no, or even hesitated over the above questions, then this book is your lifeline. Leslie Godwin's insight and depth of knowledge into what drives us to live life as though we are trapped on a perpetual tread-mill is nothing short of life changing. You owe it to yourself and to those you love to read this book."

—Dr. Greg Cynaumon
author and radio show host

"Written by an eminently wise therapist and transition coach, this is a must-read for anyone who wants to achieve life balance. It is authentic, hard-hitting and practical. It not only tells you what the problem is but, more important, WHAT TO DO ABOUT IT. The section on Creating Your Synergy Plan is priceless, as is the material on how to get out of a toxic situation."

—Clinton W. McLemore
president of RELATIONAL DYNAMICS, Inc.
author of *Street-Smart Ethics* and
Toxic Relationships and How to Change Them

"*From Burned Out to Fired Up* will speak to those who are not just frantic to get out of their current situation, but who also want to use their burnout or dissatisfaction as a wake-up call to a more meaningful life. Leslie's book is written from a deeper place than most self-help books. She has obviously been through her own journey and can take the reader where she's been, as she's done with coaching clients in her practice."

—August Turak
founder of the Self Knowledge Symposium Foundation,
Raleigh Group International, Inc.
and Elsinore Technologies, Inc.

"*From Burned Out to Fired Up* goes well beyond the popular books on burnout and following a calling. This book has it all— practical suggestions, easy-to-use worksheets, and self-assessment activities that give a deeper understanding of these issues. Author Leslie Godwin knows what she's talking about, and readers will appreciate her friendly tone. *From Burned Out to Fired Up* is just what I've been looking for to share with friends, clients and colleagues who are struggling with burnout and need to find the right career path, and, perhaps even more important, a relationship with work that won't burn them out again!"

—Mariaemma Pelullo-Willis, M.S.
Learning-Success™ coach,
co-author, *Discover Your Child's Learning Style*,
Power of You Now!™ Seminars

from
burned out
to *fired up*

A Woman's Guide to Rekindling the Passion and Meaning in Work and Life

Leslie Godwin, MFCC

Health Communications, Inc.
Deerfield Beach, Florida

www.hcibooks.com

While this book is intended to be a catalyst for positive change, if you or some-one you love is seriously burned out or depressed it may be wise to consult with a professional, since this book is not intended to replace professional treatment.

Excerpt from *INNER CHRISTIANITY* by Richard Smoley.
©2002 by Richard Smoley. Reprinted by arrangement with Shambhala Publications, Inc., Boston, *www.shambhala.com*.

Library of Congress Cataloging-in-Publication Data

Godwin, Leslie
    From burned out to fired up : a woman's guide to rekindling the passion and meaning in work and life / Leslie Godwin.
        p. cm.
    Includes bibliographical references.
    ISBN 0-7573-0195-9
    1. Women—Psychology. 2. Women—Employment—Psychological aspects.
3. Women—Conduct of life. 4. Burn out (Psychology). 5. Self-realization in women. I. Title.

HQ1206.G665 2004
646.7'0082—dc22

                                                        2004040591

©2004 Leslie Godwin
ISBN 0-7573-0195-9

HCI, its Logos and Marks are trademarks of Health Communications, Inc.

Publisher: Health Communications, Inc.
            3201 S.W. 15th Street
            Deerfield Beach, FL 33442-8190

Cover and inside book design by Lawna Patterson Oldfield
Cover photo ©Ron Chapple/PictureQuest

To S.A. and T.M.

To my husband, Bob,
thank you for always pointing me
toward something higher.

In memory of my sister,
KT Morris Samuels

CONTENTS

Chapter Seven: Your Synergy Plan Allows You to Identify and Resolve Hidden Conflicts 187

Chapter Eight: The Path Is the Goal 221

PART FOUR: REACH HIGHER

ACKNOWLEDGMENTS

Aya Dinning first heard me think out loud about writing this book and suggested I do it. So I did. Since then, many others have graciously helped me.

Among those who read my less than stellar early drafts and helped me improve them are: Jane Ahlman, Jenny Doelling, Judy Friedman, Wendy Keller, Dr. Gerry Leuthy, Catherine Valeriote and Julia Wilkinson.

Thank you to writing teacher and author, Cork Millner. I took his class, "Write From the Start" (based on his helpful book of the same title), at the Santa Barbara Adult Ed. class at the Schott Center at least three times, and I'll be back again.

Special thanks to my writing group: Judith Fraser, Julie Brams-Prudeaux, Bekah Wright, and former members Stephanie Bien, Lori Landeau and Marilyn Wedge for honest and helpful feedback.

Thank you to Dr. Laura for allowing me to contribute articles to her Web site, www.drlaura.com. Thanks to her Webmaster, Sandy Hall, and her producer, Michelle Anton.

No longer online, www.WomenCONNECT.com (and Julia Wilkinson) gave me a forum to clarify and express my thoughts, and an audience of professional women to interact with and learn from.

A most grateful thank you to my clients. Some of the examples in the book that don't include last names are composites of real people I've worked with, whom I've blended together or whose identity I otherwise altered to protect their confidentiality. Others are quotes from individuals who wished to remain anonymous. I am grateful for the opportunity to pursue my calling by serving you. I also want to thank those who e-mailed me with their stories, questions and feedback.

Thanks to the experts who allowed me to interview them.

My mother, Sue Morris, has been a wonderful draft reviewer and proofreader.

My father, Dick Morris, has given me valuable feedback on business issues.

Thank you both for your support.

My sister, KT Morris Samuels, to whom the book is dedicated, gave me great advice on many aspects of the book. She was never too busy to offer helpful suggestions and encouragement.

Special thanks to my agent, Pamela Harty with the Knight Agency. She's done more for a first-time author than I had any reason to expect was possible. I'm blessed to work with her.

Thanks to Allison Janse, my editor at HCI, Inc. Allison's suggestions were always on target and her tone supportive. The experience of working with her was better than my most optimistic idea of what it would be like, and the book is much better thanks to her help. Thanks also to Genene Hirschhorn for her expert proofreading.

Thanks to S.A. and T.M. for everything else.

INTRODUCTION

Joline is so busy at an accounting job she doesn't like, she has no time to look for a career she'll really enjoy. Occasionally, she feels so frustrated and depleted that she vows to start looking for more meaningful work. But after making some gestures toward finding another job, she gets a little anxious about actually leaving the security of her position and puts off taking action for a little while longer.

Diane always dreamed of owning a café. She finally opened her business six months ago in a space she'd had her heart set on for months. Unfortunately, what she thought would be enriching evenings spent chatting with interesting customers about music and art turned out to be frantic days spent poring over paperwork, agonizing over whether she can cover last month's bills. Once her day job is done, she spends an exhausting evening as hostess, waitress and bus-woman. She wonders if she should just cut her losses and give up. Her family hopes she will do exactly that. On the rare occasions that she's home when her family is awake, she's drained and moody.

Estee's two boys are finally in middle school, and she can't wait to do something fun, satisfying and profitable with her newfound time. If she only knew what that might be. When she was younger, she thought about being a teacher. Now she's not so sure. How does she begin to discover her calling and how to act on it?

Like these women, you may be considering changing careers to:

- get out of a frustrating job that's draining your energy and creativity
- gain control of your schedule
- make time for children and other important family commitments
- stop living crisis to crisis
- do something that allows you to express your true self

Without a map and a guide, it's hard to know where to start. Many women who dream of leaving a frustrating job, or who are ready to get into the workforce after raising a family, aren't sure how to approach finding their perfect career. Some try to fit themselves into an available position, but end up settling for a job that doesn't allow them the self-expression they had hoped for. Others start up their own business, assuming that if they were their own boss, they'd control their schedule and do things their way. Unfortunately, many female entrepreneurs become slaves to their own businesses.

What's the point of having a plan that ensures cash flow for the business but prevents you from realizing the dreams and priorities that make your life worth living? Or one that encourages you to dream about the day you'll be spiritually fulfilled but doesn't offer a clue about how to make that happen? As a psychotherapist and a career and life-transition coach, I specialize in creating strategies that enable clients to successfully combine their gifts and talents with their values and priorities. I also help clients use life transitions—including crises like burnout or job loss—to deepen their understanding of themselves and their place in the world. For years, I searched in vain for a book that each of my clients could use—a guide to developing career strategies and business plans that integrates their personal goals and family's needs. I realized that I had to write the book I wanted to share with them, and the book I wished I'd had when I was burned out.

What's in It for You?

This book will help you find and follow your calling, whether you want to start your own business or you just feel like there's something missing in your life. Using the worksheets and journaling exercises, you'll create a detailed map built on the solid foundation of your values, priorities, and family and personal responsibilities. I call this map a "Synergy Plan" because it integrates all of these important elements with career planning and goals.

Many women have used this process, and in doing so, have found their calling in once-chaotic lives. By learning where to focus their energy, they're now more fulfilled and less frazzled; more energized and less stressed. They've let go of the guilt they used to feel because they knew in their hearts that they weren't living according to what was most important to them.

You can read this book from beginning to end or you can skip around. Part One includes a quiz you can take to see if you're burned out. If so, you'll learn how you got that way and what you need to do to reorganize your life around a higher purpose. Part Two spells out four types of burnout I've come across in my work (and in myself) and what you can do about them. Part Three gives step-by-step guidance to reprioritize your life and live according to your values. And Part Four will help you stay on your true path over the long-term.

Keep a Journal

To make your time spent reading this book more productive, keep a journal or notebook. You can use this not only to answer various questions in the journaling exercises at the end of most chapters, but also to articulate where you feel stuck and what to do about it.

Do you fantasize about a time in the future when you are doing just what you want—doing what you are *meant* to do? You can do something about it right now. Chapter 1 will help you start at the beginning with understanding what a calling is, and how to find yours.

We don't receive wisdom;
we must discover it for ourselves
after a journey that no one can
take for us or spare us.
—MARCEL PROUST

PART ONE

BECOMING INWARDLY MOBILE

CHAPTER ONE

You Have a Calling: Are You Listening?

"Don't ask yourself what the world needs.
Ask yourself what makes you come alive, and go
do that, because what the world needs
is people who have come alive."

—GIL BAILIE

Terry, a financial consultant, is either handling a client crisis or recovering from the last one. She spends most of her day rushing from cell phone call to her computer, faxing documents as she runs out of the office on the way to handle the next emergency. Terry tells me, "I used to feel so alive and useful going from one frantic situation to the next. Now I just feel drained."

Joan, a marketing expert and mother of two, explains, "You know that feeling you get when you've slept an hour too late and you're running an hour behind all day long, trying to catch up? I feel like that everyday. I have more to do than I can physically get done, and I can't remember the last time I was able to relax and just enjoy the moment. I'm not moving toward my goals, I'm just barely getting through the day."

Seeing Burnout as a Gift

Feeling exhausted and that your life lacks purpose or focus doesn't feel like a gift. Yet, if being burned out provides you with the motivation to reexamine your life, not simply to make slight adjustments so you can return to your previous life with a little less pain, then it's a priceless gift.

You can push yourself to reach external goals for years, never acknowledging that you're not on your true path. Until one day you hit the wall—you become physically ill, you lose it at the supermarket as you rush to buy dinner on your way home or you just "know" as you walk into your office with a feeling of dread that you can't continue with business as usual, ignoring essential parts of yourself and your life. That's what happened to Elaine.

Elaine has been a performer since she was sixteen. She modeled, did improv, and did some acting. But mostly she worked on the road as a professional comic. "I'd be on the road for four and five months at a time. I lived like that for years. For about three of those years, I didn't even have a home. I slept on people's couches when I was in town for a few days to a couple of weeks."

About eight or nine years into her career, when she was finally headlining at well-known clubs, Elaine hit the wall, completely burned out from all the stress, travel and just the lifestyle of being on the road all the time. "I actually lost my voice and couldn't talk for three weeks. That woke me up. I realized that I just couldn't do that anymore."

Because Elaine saw her crisis as a wake-up call and didn't just regroup for another try at success as a performer, she was able to change her course. It wasn't an easy transformation. All she knew was performing. "I had no idea what else I could do, and I didn't have any real job skills. So I had a conversation with God. I said, 'I can't live like this. Show me what I can do that won't steal my soul.' I looked at the want ads for the first time in my life. They seemed like they were in another language. I saw an ad in the paper that said, 'Dog Trainers Wanted'. I got the job and trained dogs for that company for about six years. I discovered that I was actually good at it.

"Everything I did prior to dog training was about furthering my career. I never had a hobby until I started training dogs for protection sports. I never went to dinner to just go to dinner. It was all networking. I got a life and found out that I was good at something else besides performing." About four years ago, Elaine went out on her own and started Canine's Best Behavior. "Performing never seemed like a meaningful job to me. Training dogs to have a better relationship with their owners, and training detection dogs who will sniff out explosives and dogs who chase down bad guys, makes me feel I'm contributing something valuable to society."

If Elaine hadn't gotten so burned out, she might have continued chasing external success as a stand-up comic for years, even though it wasn't fulfilling to her and it clearly didn't allow her to create a home and grounded life for herself. Her burnout crisis, and her courage to use her crisis as a wake-up call, was a life-changing gift.

Why Do We Need a Crisis to Get Out of Our Ruts?

For many of us, nothing short of hitting the wall can convince us to let go of our unsatisfying, but familiar, careers and lives, and ask for guidance. But, if our lives are unfulfilling and lack meaning and passion, why do we need a crisis of any kind, much less one as debilitating as being burned out, to get our lives back on track? I have two answers to that question.

1. Because our nature is such that when we're shaken up, we first make small adjustments to keep the status quo. Most of us don't instantly upend our lives every time we're in a bad mood. (There's a mental health diagnosis for that disorder, since turning our lives upside down without good reason makes it hard to function.)

2. We grow up believing certain myths that become engrained in our psyche and can lead to burnout. By "myth" I don't mean fables from ancient times. I mean those truisms that help define and describe some of the ideals of a culture. But some of these myths keep us from discovering who we're meant to become as individuals. This is understandable, because myths and the cultures they describe are for the benefit of the group, not the individual.

A crisis provides us one of the few opportunities we have to break free from the hypnotic trance of these myths.

The Four Myths That Lead to Burnout

Are any of these myths familiar to you?

- Myth One: Work Hard Now, Enjoy Yourself Later
- Myth Two: Make Sure You Keep Your Life "Under Control"
- Myth Three: Grown-Ups Should Know What They Want to Do with Their Lives
- Myth Four: Upward Mobility Is Better Than Inward Mobility

Myth One: Work Hard Now, Enjoy Yourself Later

This sounds so logical, and so practical. It even allows for fun, as long as you wait until later, when you deserve it. Unfortunately, later never comes.

A basic flaw of this myth is the separation of work and enjoyment. When you were growing up your mother may have nagged, "Do your homework before you go out and play," or, "Don't forget to do your yardwork before you watch TV." Not only may the latter have discouraged you from enjoying gardening later in life because you still see it as a chore, but the principles underlying these common instructions are designed to promote willpower over enjoyment.

Willpower is useful at times. I use willpower to get the garbage out on Friday mornings. But there's a price to pay for relying on willpower. Using willpower is the opposite of using your imagination and of losing yourself in an activity. Willpower reduces any activity to the very low status of "chore." The older you get, the less you get to "play" and get back in touch with that timeless feeling of being fully engaged in the present, even after your chores are done. What remains is the illusion that your day consists of a list of chores, and that if you could only check them all off your list, you'd be able to enjoy some peace and quiet, read that book you've been meaning to start or pursue a fun project or hobby.

The more your life is structured around chores, and the more the pleasures of play are hermetically sealed in an imaginary container labeled, "Open when your chores are finished," the less likely you are to ever reach them.

Most of us have unconsciously accepted the idea that chores and work are responsible adult activities and play is something done when you're not in the "real world," like when you're on vacation (which I'll get to in a moment). This structure separates and polarizes the concepts of work and play. It excludes the possibility of finding joy in everyday life and bringing a playful feeling to all you do.

Vacations

Vacations reinforce this myth that life will start once your chores are done. Once or twice a year you take a vacation. This typically involves working like crazy until it's time to get ready— frantically packing, helping family members pack, arranging for pets to be taken care of and, of course, reviewing your checklist of things to be done before your trip. Then you waste the day at the airport and then crowd into an airplane, or you pack up the car and spend a day or more getting to where this fun and relaxation is supposed to happen. Once there, you unwind for half a day, nap and finally relax.

One reason we're better able to relax on vacation is that we have few reminders of our normal day-to-day tasks that keep our minds busy (unless we're really struggling with the concept of getting away and bring our cell phone and laptop, or work-related reading and reports to write.) And our environment looks different, which gets our attention and enhances our enjoyment of walking, exploring and eating in new restaurants.

After a day or two, you actually begin to enjoy yourself and live in the moment. You've worked hard and earned time off, so you probably don't even feel guilty about not being "productive." You remember why you married your husband. You remember why you love your kids. You may even get a glimpse of what you'd love to do with your life, but you quickly add the mental comment, "someday" or "in another life" to distinguish between what must be fantasy and "real life."

Now it's time to pack up and get back home. You take one last look around at the view from your hotel and vow to bring this inspired and grounded feeling back home with you. You pack and feel it slipping slowly away as you take care of the chores you do when a vacation comes to an end—pay the bill, return your room key, check the drawers and shower for items you may have left behind, and get the car packed up. You can still conjure up the relaxed feeling, though, and remind yourself to calm down when there's a line to check out of the hotel.

But by the time you're in the airport, or have driven half an hour, that relaxed feeling begins slipping away for good. You get out of the present moment and start creating a new checklist:

- get the dog from the sitter or kennel
- water the lawn
- put out the garbage
- unpack and do the laundry
- make sure the kids' stuff is ready for school tomorrow
- figure out what to do for dinner

After you get home and check off all those items, then you can read the book you enjoyed so much on vacation or watch TV.

In other words, you're right back where you started.

If you aren't in the process of developing a rich internal world, and you use vacations as an escape from your day-to-day life, those moments of escape give you the illusion of freedom. That's how vacations can keep you enslaved.

It Takes Practice to Enjoy Life Fully

How can you become more skilled at any activity without time or effort spent honing that skill? Enjoying your life and appreciating what you already have is a skill that takes lots of practice as well as some self-discipline. The more you practice valuing exactly what you have this very moment, the more likely you are to excel at doing so in the future.

Alan Watts, a philosopher and speaker known for his ability to express complicated truths in a compelling way, had this to say about living for the future:

> Memories of the past and anticipation of the future are not other moments, but parts of this one. . . . The thought that there is just this moment, and no other one, is at first sight against all common sense. It seems so completely obvious that there most certainly will be other moments, that tomorrow will soon be here, with the very concrete reality of its work to be done, and its pains and travails to be suffered. True. But if you look at the matter clearly, it becomes quite obvious that you cannot experience any other moment than this one with any degree of vivid reality.[1]

---

[1]Watts, Alan. *Talking Zen*. New York: Weatherhill, 1994. pp. 82–83.

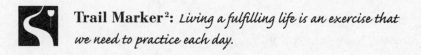

Trail Marker[2]: *Living a fulfilling life is an exercise that we need to practice each day.*

Myth Two: Make Sure You Keep Your Life "Under Control"

"I have been terribly fearful of losing financial security as well as the emotional security of a relationship," tells Cathy, a fifty-something woman whose life revolved around staying in control. "I couldn't take chances. And what happened? I found I couldn't control others, and what I feared most would happen, did. My husband walked out on me. My fears and insecurities played a big role in this. Wow! That took me a lot of therapy sessions to admit.

"Most of all I felt fear . . . fear of life . . . fear of change."

It took Cathy a long time to realize that her need to be in control was based on fear. Giving up the illusion of being in control is one of the hardest steps toward following your calling and getting in touch with your true self. Maybe the first step is to notice that feeling in control of your life is more often an illusion than it is a reality.

Many women understand Cathy's feeling of dread about losing control. For many of us, our roles in life seem to be to take charge and be responsible. Other people's moods, behavior and their ultimate happiness are some of the areas in which we feel we can make a difference. You may feel that you can cheer up a friend's bad mood or that your advice to a family member will give them just

---

[2]*Trail Markers let us know when we're beginning to stray off our path and help us find our paths when we are feeling lost. I use this term for occasional tips you'll find within the text.*

the insight they need to stop a lifelong bad habit. If a coworker doesn't like you, you may assume it's because you aren't being charming or reasonable enough with them. It can be hard to deeply grasp the concept that we can only do our part, and then the free will of others takes over. But it's only when we let go of our need to feel in control of others that we can discover who we are underneath our fears and compulsive behaviors.

Another way to put our lives in perspective is to think about what we *can't* control. What do you think about when you look up at the star-filled sky at night? Try looking at the vast expanse of the starry sky, and contemplate how small you are in comparison. Then, see if you can identify with the vastness you see above. We're each a tiny speck in the universe *and* an integral part of that vastness. We're just one little piece of a vast puzzle.

Myth Three: Grown-Ups Should Know What They Want to Do with Their Lives

I hear from a lot of women and men who want to make a change but who are ashamed or embarrassed that they don't know what they want to do at this point in their lives. Their embarrassment is based on the misguided idea that they should already know something so basic about themselves.

The Cure for Believing You Should Know What You Want to Do with Your Life

The ability to ask a good question, yet not rush in with an answer, is the cure for feeling you should know it all. Instead of allowing your ego to feel puffed up with how much you know, or of being ashamed that you feel lost, allow your true self to open up to what you *don't know* and make room for deeper and more profound answers.

If you're stuck in feelings of shame, discomfort or other angst about not knowing what you want to do with your life, you have to stop reacting and start responding to those feelings differently. This is different than trying to push down the feelings. You'll still have your feelings. You just won't be allowing them to boss you around. You can only find something out by first *not knowing*. (Tell that to the part of yourself that is badgering you!)

This works with other important questions in life besides career choices. Let's say you're worried about your daughter. She seems angry a lot of the time, and you don't understand why. Your first reaction may be to want to rescue her from her feelings, which is a natural maternal reaction. Or you may hope that if you don't pay too much attention to it, she'll grow out of it. But these reactions are based on fear and anxiety, not wisdom.

If you allow yourself to wonder why she's so angry, you'll eventually understand her better. And you'll discover the right way to handle the situation. You'll probably be led to ask her about her feelings; when they began, what she feels like and if her feelings scare her at all. You'll show your daughter that you're concerned, without alienating her further. She'll notice your calm way of trying to make sense of something that is very upsetting to both of you. At some point, by giving up the idea that you *know* what to do, you'll *find out* what to do. And you will have shown your daughter how to handle upsetting and difficult problems by your example.

So, open your mind and ask yourself some good questions, and let the answers come when they're ready.

One of the barriers to discovering who you are and what you're supposed to be doing is to assume that you already know all that.

The more you know, the less you'll discover. An example that makes this point is the story about the Zen master pouring tea for his student. The student finally has a chance to meet with this famous Zen master to ask some questions about what he is supposed to do with his life. They both sit down for tea and to talk. The master starts pouring tea, and the student watches his every move very carefully, excited to finally be in the presence of this wise person. The master fills the cup, but then keeps pouring.

After watching the tea pour all over the table and onto the floor, the student is getting very uncomfortable. The tea keeps coming, and the cup is really overflowing. Finally the student can't keep from saying something, so he asks, "Why are you pouring all that tea, when the cup is already full?" The master says, "That overfull cup is like your overfull mind. There is no room for me to add anything. You have to empty your mind if you want to take in anything I have to offer you."

Our human nature makes us feel that truly having an open mind is not an asset. Our need to constantly find problems to solve is one aspect of our nature more suited to maintaining the status quo than to living a meaningful life. So we scan the horizon for clues, we think about everything we already know about the subject, we try to remember what has worked for others we know, and we consider what is the easiest way to accomplish our goal that would cause the least disruption in our lives. We do everything *but* empty our minds to discover our own answer, which comes from a deeper place inside us that is not concerned with mere *survival* but with *growth*.

Myth Four: Upward Mobility Is Better Than Inward Mobility

The term "upwardly mobile" defined a generation of external achievers. I call those of us aspiring to listen to our inner voice or calling and determined to become who we are meant to be, "inwardly mobile."

Accomplishments and *outward* successes are easy to share with friends and family. You'll probably get praise and admiration, and maybe even some envy from others. They'll know just what you're talking about, and they'll have an elaborate context for the information. It will have meaning, value and interest to them.

On the other hand, becoming a deeper person and having a richer, more meaningful *interior* life seems almost invisible to people who are focused on the external world. Most people assume that living a meaningful life will occur on its own sometime between now and retirement, or at least before they die. Yet, one day something shifts slightly, and they start to feel uncomfortable. A friend dies too young, a neighbor's child gets hit by a car, their children grow up and don't need them as much in the way that made them feel that they had an essential job to do. Soon they see through this myth. But then what do they do?

How can we impress people if we don't succeed in a way that they value? And how can we make our goals a top priority when they are only a blip on the radar to most people we care about? When it comes to our inner workings, most people are inarticulate—even ignorant—about what goes on. Focusing on our inner world may be a fairly lonely experience, especially if we require a lot of encouragement and acknowledgment from others. Or if we still aim to please our family or need their approval consciously or unconsciously.

I felt like I was living in a fog all those years in terms of knowing what I wanted to do with my life. When the fog lifted, I didn't even know where my path was, *much less how to get on it.*

—JACKIE, THIRTY-TWO-YEAR-OLD CUSTOMER
SERVICE REPRESENTATIVE AND MOTHER OF TWO

There are very few of us who are "called" so forcefully early in life that we live our entire lives responding to that call. That means that most of us go along living our lives in a semi-aware fog until somehow the question "What am I doing with my life?" comes into sharp focus.

Colin Wilson writes that Rudolf Steiner ". . . never ceased to try to explain to his fellow men: You are mistaken to treat the 'world of the mind' as if it were merely a metaphor, or a dim reflection of the physical world. It is *another country,* and we all have passports to cross into it."[3]

This feeling that the "world of the mind" isn't quite as real as the physical world is probably why most people wait until at least midlife to launch into inner life exploration. At that point their quality of life is significantly more important than what others think of them. Much of this book has to do with speeding up the process of caring less what others think of you, and more about the quality of your life. And quality of life happens mostly on the inside.

Another way you can lose touch with your inner world and true self is to live a hectic life. Does your life usually move at a frenetic

---

[3] Wilson, Colin. *Rudolf Steiner: The Man and His Vision. An Introduction to the Life and Ideas of the Founder of Anthroposophy.* Northamptonshire: The Quarian Press, 1985. p. 77.

pace? Is your baseline level of activity just short of frantic? Do you ever feel like you can't add one more thing to your normal schedule? If so, you may have become desensitized to your high level of activity, and you see it as acceptable or, at least, unavoidable. Or you may have an unconscious need to stay busy. Unfortunately, you pay a price for being so busy. The busier you are addressing outside commitments, the less of an internal life you allow yourself. And cultivating your internal life is part of the preparation for hearing your calling.

Numerous practical problems also arise from living a hectic lifestyle. One is that after years of living this way, you may be used to the pace and to doing things yourself as opposed to delegating. In other words, you've developed habits that are hard to break. Another problem is that you've committed yourself to obligations and responsibilities that don't go away when you decide to live more simply. So you have two problems to face: breaking ingrained habits, and then extricating yourself from the results of past choices.

Our Culture Isn't Supposed to Encourage Our Emergence as Individuals

The fact that our culture supports upward mobility and not inward mobility is not some kind of evil conspiracy to keep us from fully becoming who we are meant to be. As I pointed out earlier, the job of any culture is *not* to produce unique individuals. It is to produce a group that shares certain values and concerns. Mihaly Csikszentmihalyi, a professor and author who has devoted his life's work to the study of what makes people truly happy, satisfied and fulfilled, says that, "Just as genes use the body as a vehicle for their own reproduction, a culture also tends to use individuals as vehicles for its own survival and growth."[4] My husband told me once that you don't need a lid on a bucket of live crabs to keep them all in the bucket. They keep each other in the bucket. If one tries to climb out, the others grab him and pull him back in. Are you in a bucket of crabs trying to get out? Who is keeping you in? Do you feel it is your parents? Your husband? Your culture? Or is it a part of you that wants to stay stuck where you are?

For most of us those confining messages are only echoes, not the original voice. We hear them and blame them for enslaving us. But, once you reach adulthood and have lived on your own for several years, it's your own doing if you keep yourself locked into what is familiar. At that point, you have internalized your family's values and fears, and your culture's rules and limits to individual freedom. You could change your surroundings, but you would still take along your version of what is blocking you. We're all profoundly affected by our families and environment, but the trick is to evolve beyond external limitations and find our own way of understanding the meaning of our lives. (I'll say more about the effect of our family and culture in the discussion in chapter 2 about the type of burnout that's caused by reacting to, or trying to please, others.)

Colin Wilson writes in the postscript to the biography of Rudolf Steiner mentioned earlier, "[Steiner] is saying, in effect: the bird is a creature of the air; the fish is a creature of the water; the worm is a creature of the earth. But man is essentially a *creature of the mind*. His true home is a world inside himself. It is true that we have to live in the external world; but . . . we have to retreat inside ourselves if we are to grasp this outer world."

---

[4]Csikszentmihalyi, Mihaly. *The Evolving Self*. New York: HarperCollins, 1993. p. 71.

The Inwardly Mobile Woman
Listens to Her Calling

In the attitude of silence the soul
finds the path in a clearer light, and what
is elusive and deceptive resolves itself into
crystal clearness. Our life is a long
and arduous quest after Truth.

—Mahatma Gandhi

What is a calling? Will God speak to me and instruct me in some direct and visible way? Or is a calling the same as my intuition? Will listening to it change me from being logical and practical and turn me into a flaky do-gooder led around by my feelings? If I listen to my calling, will I have to leave my worldly possessions and family behind to go on a quest to some faraway primitive place to find enlightenment and live out my days chopping wood and chanting a mantra?

These are the questions that come to mind for many of us when we think about following a calling. Maybe we associate following a calling with hippies in the late 1960s and early 1970s who were striving for some magical, conflict-free lifestyle as part of their search for identity. Some of them may have been following a true calling; others may have accidentally stumbled upon a method that worked for them. Most of them, though, were conformists following the pack, and that was what a certain pack was doing at that time.

Had they come of age now, their ritual may have been to get a sensitive body part pierced or to wear pants three times too big.

There can be a genuine aspect of seeking self-understanding underneath all this conformity, but most young people aren't able to separate out the needs of their soul from the needs of their egos. Or their need to individuate from their family's values and find out who they are. But they don't usually get any closer to the truth about themselves in these ways.

Understanding Your Calling Means Understanding Who You Really Are

A calling is very personal, yet there are universal aspects to listening to and following our calling. I think of a calling as what you intuit when you tune into your true or authentic self. Our true self is not our external personality that we use to present ourselves to the world. Neither is it what we wish we were. It's something very pure. It's a spark inside us that makes us want to know ourselves in a deeper way. We've all met people with a special quality that makes them seem more alive than other people. They are people who don't seem to get sidetracked by a need for recognition, material success, or to be part of a certain social group. They're able to see the extraordinary in the ordinary, and don't limit themselves with popular ideas about what's the right car to drive, how their home should be decorated or any other man-made value. Instead, they are self-actualized in the sense that they value their true self, have identified their calling, and live according to their deepest held beliefs and values.

Countless myths, folktales, books and movies portray the tragedy of ignoring one's calling. The hero is full of talent and ambition, but life provides him with a series of unexpected events that create a completely different scenario than the one he anticipated. He now has so many practical burdens that his talents and dreams wither from neglect, and he becomes old and bitter. Often these tales include some kind of wake-up call that forces our hero to reconsider his path in life and turn once again toward his dreams. This rebirth into his authentic self is what saves him, and his life becomes rich with meaning.

How Do I Hear My Calling in the Chaos?

People get in such ruts, and get stuck in their "comfort zones." The initial work and risk it takes to get into your true calling is scary, and people need to get past that.

—Julia Wilkinson
author of *Best Bang for Your Book*

In our busy daily lives, we don't think too much about our calling, or about getting in touch with our true selves. Most of us are simply trying to get through each day, check off as many items on our to-do lists as possible and take care of our family's and our own physical needs. We get up, gulp down some coffee, grab some breakfast, rush to work, keep up this pace when we get to work, pick up some dinner on the way home and wash the dishes before going to bed. If we're married, add a few items to this list. If we have children, add some more to include their needs, wants and maybe some time for family fun. Who has time or energy to create an internal dialogue, when the outside world and its demands are hounding us throughout the day?

One of the reasons that many religions and spiritual traditions consider the latter third of life as the proper time to turn inward and live a life according to their spiritual teachings is that until that point, the noise of the outside world is so loud it drowns out our quiet inner voice. And coping with day-to-day life doesn't leave enough time or energy for most people to stay focused on this inner world. When we're young, we're initiated into our family and our culture. When we're in our middle years of developing a career, creating a life with a spouse and, in many cases, parenting, we typically don't have the burning desire to pursue a more inward path. But once these worldly activities aren't as consuming, we have more and more glimpses that these usual ways of getting our needs met have left an unnamed part of us unfulfilled. That is often the impetus that sparks us to consider turning inward and getting to know our true selves better.

Harry Moody, Ph.D., author of *The Five Stages of the Soul*, has found that "Women, it seems, as they answer the Call, often feel the need to disentangle from overidentification with family, friends, [and] loved ones. . . ."[5] Men have their own challenges when they try to become more authentic, but we women usually define ourselves by the way we fit into others' lives. There's nothing wrong with acknowledging where we fit into the lives of those we care about. But if we don't put the focus on discovering our true selves, we risk getting stuck identifying with one of our roles when we need to look deeper to understand who we are underneath those roles, our social persona and how we respond to what others need and expect from us. This is exactly what

> Women, it seems, as they answer the Call, often feel the need to disentangle from overidentification with family, friends, [and] loved ones.

---

[5]Harry Moody, Ph.D. *The Five Stages of the Soul*. New York: Anchor Books/Doubleday: 1997, p. 109.

happened to Judith, who used the comfort zone of her mother role to avoid discovering other parts of her true self. She explains:

> *I had been feeling anxious about my life. My children were growing up, my chosen career of acting wasn't fruitful, and something inside of me that I call my "inner wisdom" created such a sense of anxiety that I had to pay attention to it. I went to see a psychologist and while working with him I knew that I could do what he was doing.*
>
> *It hit me like a bolt of lightening. The consequences were that I had to change my life. I had to let go of working in theater, being overly available to my husband and children, (to say nothing about being available to every neighborhood child who needed a surrogate parent) and focus on me. I had been overindulging my family to avoid figuring out what I wanted to do with my life.*
>
> *— Judith Fraser* *(Please see p. 274 for the rest of her story)*

Retreating inward to get in touch with our true selves can appear as though we're being selfish or avoiding our responsibilities. (And it's possible to be exactly that, especially if we retreat from our role as wife, or mother of children still living at home.) Eventually, after disentangling from overidentification with these roles, as Dr. Moody calls it, we can simply be ourselves. Then we're free to reenter these roles with the clear vision of who we are underneath them.

What if You Did Know?

It's hard at first to get in touch with our true selves when we need to respond quickly to a question from our child, an invitation from an acquaintance or to a crisis at work. We're used to respond-ing based on our feelings, what others want to hear or what will cause us the least pain or effort.

Dr. Laura Schlessinger, the radio personality well-known for helping callers with their moral dilemmas, has a technique that helps callers respond from this unfamiliar part of themselves, usu-ally without their knowing it. Dr. Laura has a gift for getting to the heart of a dilemma. But callers can shrink from her direct questions and often tell her that they "don't know" the answer she's looking for. Dr. Laura often responds, "If you did know, what would the answer be?" I've only once heard a caller stick with the "I don't know" response after being encouraged to put their truth into words. Every other caller that I've heard has managed to reply in some way, and they continue the conversation on a deeper level.

Trail Marker: *Try asking yourself, "What if I did know?" the next time you're struggling with a decision or trying to make sense of a hunch about a person or situation.*

The part of you that responds to this demand to speak "as if you did know," is your true self. So how do you get in touch with that part of you at will? And how do you stay in touch with her all of the time? An important part of that process of tuning in to our true self includes quieting the background noise in our lives that drowns out the sound of our true voice or calling.

Journaling Exercise

Use this method when you need an answer to a question that begins with: "What should I do about . . . ?"

1. Start by assuming that there is a quiet voice inside you that speaks for your true self.

2. Ask yourself a question. For instance:
What is my calling?
Is my job crushing my soul?
If the problem isn't my job, why aren't I in touch with my true self?
What am I avoiding by staying on the surface of life? By staying so busy?

3. Clear your mind of all existing assumptions and chatter. Be firm with yourself. Ignore the chatter when it tries to get your attention.

4. Wait patiently, knowing an answer will come. If you press for an answer, you'll get back into your usual way of thinking.

5. If you still draw a blank, tell yourself that an answer will come. This isn't a job for your conscious thought process. If you believe in God or a Higher Power, ask for His help and be open to His message.

At first you might feel that you're crazy trying to listen to something that may not even be there or is so quiet you can't tell if it's saying one thing or something completely different.

It's like listening to a shy little girl who wants you to hear her but is afraid that you may not like what she has to say. She speaks so quietly that she's barely audible. You may completely misunderstand her if you're not listening carefully. You may be tempted to talk for her to spare her the effort, but then it's you again in charge—the external you. So you keep trying to draw her out, to repeat back what you think she said to see if you got it right, to let her know you really want to hear what she has to say.

Then a shift takes place in the relationship. Pretty soon, she isn't so shy around you at all. She talks to you about whatever's on her mind. She's no longer barely audible, but speaks clearly and confidently. She may become shy again around other people, especially those who don't make the effort to get to know her as you did. But with your encouragement, she may overcome her shyness even in those challenging situations.

If you're consistent, and sincerely curious about discovering more and more about your true self, you'll develop a real relationship with that part of yourself. You may lose touch with your true self when you're really stressed or when you're around others who intimidate you. But with persistence and confidence, that also can be resolved.

Make Sure Your Ladder Is Against the Right Wall

There is an expression that asks, "What if you spend your whole life climbing a ladder only to find that it is against the wrong wall?" If you're not following your calling, or if you simply don't know what your calling is yet, it's scary to decide to get off the wrong trail, because you've already invested so much hard work. When I talk to clients about this I sometimes use the image of getting lost while driving. We've all had the feeling at some point when trying to find a location for the first time, "What if I am going the wrong way?" Even though it seems foolish to continue on, we hesitate to turn around because we've already gone so far. Once we've invested so much, no matter how illogical it is to continue on the wrong path, it seems a waste to give up. Only when you're finally on the right track do you realize how much time, energy and resources you've wasted on the wrong paths.

"If you've had a certain level of success in something, it's hard to step away from that ride even if you're not crazy about it," tells Margot Lester, president of The Word Factory. "Partly because of what other people will think, and also because you're stepping away from what has given you self-esteem."

If I'd written this book several years ago, I would have offered you very practical advice about how to follow someone else's dream. Of course, I wouldn't have put it that way. I would have recommended that you find a role model whose life you'd like to emulate, find out how they got there, and follow their path. When I came up with this method, I thought I'd discovered a very useful technique. I even found role models that met this description, whom I still greatly admire. I had no idea how to get my life to look more like theirs, but trying seemed very logical. Looking back, though, it seems completely absurd. Once we make a commitment to become more authentic, our colleagues, friends, family and others will show up to help us to travel further on our path. This doesn't work if we make a commitment to become like someone else. We have to give those who want to help us a clue as to what we're committed to, so they can help us to find and make use of opportunities.

I believe that the point of life is to become more ourselves and strip away whatever holds us back from that goal. This includes quieting our external-oriented minds so we can find the natural rhythm or flow of *our* path.

In the next four chapters I'll describe four types of burnout. The first is found in chapter 2, which will help you determine if you're a passionate workaholic who is fueled by emotion and adrenaline rather than following the natural flow of your career path.

Quiz

Are You Inwardly Mobile or Burned Out?

✓ 1 = Not much/Doesn't apply to me
✓ 2 = Somewhat
✓ 3 = Very much so

I like what I do, and I'm good at it, but I feel that something is missing from my life.	❑ 1	❑ 2	❑ 3
I don't have enough time for the things I value and/or enjoy most: family, hobbies, exercise, sports, community involvement, etc.	❑ 1	❑ 2	❑ 3
I don't know how I could find a job I'd love that would pay enough.	❑ 1	❑ 2	❑ 3
I don't feel I'm productive unless I'm busy.	❑ 1	❑ 2	❑ 3
I need the adrenaline "rush" that comes from getting a new client or being up against a deadline.	❑ 1	❑ 2	❑ 3
I thrive on deadlines and pressure at work.	❑ 1	❑ 2	❑ 3
My job really drains my energy.	❑ 1	❑ 2	❑ 3
I spend so much energy on work that I feel rundown quite a bit.	❑ 1	❑ 2	❑ 3
I'm reluctant to commit to a career path because I'll have to give up other possibilities.	❑ 1	❑ 2	❑ 3
I want to find the right career path, but I don't know what it is yet.	❑ 1	❑ 2	❑ 3
I don't take too many risks in my career, since I need a certain income to cover my bills.	❑ 1	❑ 2	❑ 3

I feel great on the weekend but start to feel down on Sunday night, and dread going to work Monday morning.	❏ 1	❏ 2	❏ 3
I wish I could leave, but something always comes up that keeps me at my job.	❏ 1	❏ 2	❏ 3
I want to focus on my career/grow my business, but there is never enough time.	❏ 1	❏ 2	❏ 3
I know my kids/ spouse/ parents/others need more of my time and energy, and I feel guilty I can't be more available.	❏ 1	❏ 2	❏ 3
I feel overwhelmed by the combination of work and family activities I am responsible for.	❏ 1	❏ 2	❏ 3

___ ___ ___

Score: Add up the numbers you circled

40-48: You're quite burned out and need to look inward to make a fundamental shift in your focus, put your values and priorities first, and rely on your intuition not on external triggers and emotions.

21-39: You're at risk of burnout and need to work on developing your inner life.

16-20: You're Inwardly Mobile. You don't simply react to your environment, but are grounded and use your intuition to guide you. You need to continue to hone this ability.

JOURNALING EXERCISE

1. When you look at the quiz items you checked, what is the message you get?

_____

_____

_____

2. Do you notice that you feel you have to choose between making a living and enjoying your career? (We'll address this issue in chapter 6.)

_____

_____

_____

3. Is your stress mostly related to an unpleasant job situation? (We'll discuss this in chapter 4.)

_____

_____

_____

4. Do you notice any conflicts between how you do spend your time and energy, and how you feel you should spend your time and energy? (This will be covered in chapter 7.)

_____

_____

_____

5. Do you see any obvious areas to make some changes? What are these changes?

_____

_____

_____

6. On which items did you score a 3? Without being self-critical, write down your thoughts about those statements:

_____

_____

_____

_____

_____

_____

_____

_____

_____

_____

_____

_____

_____

_____

_____

_____

PART TWO

FOUR TYPES OF BURNOUT

Type One: Passionate Workaholics— Stop Driving Yourself Crazy and Go with the Flow

"After a year the thrill, and the energy
I got from that thrill, just wasn't there anymore.
After the second year I think the only thing
that kept me going was fear. I didn't want
to be just another failed business.
Another restaurant that disappeared."

—FRAN, RESTAURATEUR

I used to think that if I poured all of my energy and enthusiasm into my work that I would not only be successful on the job, but that my work would then meet my many complicated and conflicting personal needs. It took me by surprise that this approach led me to become burned out. First, I'll tell you about how I tried to use emotion to fuel my work. Then, I'll describe what I have come to believe is a much better fuel source than emotion for your work and how it can help you avoid falling prey to this type of burnout again.

35

The Old Me: Driven and Confused

I used to feel very driven. In fact, I come from a long line of workaholics and actually aspired to be even more driven than I was. I had three part-time jobs simultaneously while I was in graduate school, yet it never occurred to me that I may not have been able to do them all well. Or that I would sacrifice any aspect of my well-being by working so many hours and studying in any remaining spare moments.

When I wasn't working, I usually felt that I was being lazy. I allowed myself some time with my boyfriend (now my husband) to have fun and relax. But overall, my life was much more centered around work than it was focused on enjoying life or reflecting on what a good life should be.

I defined myself by my job title, so I had to keep acquiring more impressive job titles to "grow" professionally. I never did feel like I was as successful as I was supposed to be. None of my bosses realized how "gifted" I was and promoted me, the golden child, to the lofty status that would assure me and the world that I was worthy.

The problem was, I was trying to discover myself from the outside-in. I assumed that I should run my life based on status reports from the outside world. That way I would know how I was doing, just like when my parents, teachers or supervisors evaluated me and critiqued my abilities and effort, or lack thereof.

I had some experience of being inner directed and had definite opinions about certain issues. But I was confused because my ego, which needed the external confirmation of job promotions, raises and praise, was louder and pushier than the part of me that was inner directed. The more I listened to my ego, the worse I felt. My ego just wanted to feel secure and to know that I was doing what was expected of me. It didn't want me to grow or to find a new way to understand life and my place in it. I didn't realize that the solution was to develop the inner-directed part.

Keep Your Arms and Legs Inside the Car
Till the Roller-Coaster Comes to a Complete Stop

Despite my darker tendencies toward workaholism, I somehow was able to develop some valuable skills and enjoyed my work a lot. Enjoy isn't the right word. I loved and needed my work. My moods and sense of well-being were completely dependent on how my worklife was going. By this time, I was running a multi-faceted program for homeless mentally ill adults and those at risk of homelessness. I got excited when a client graduated our program, and I got discouraged when we had to move someone out who needed more structure. I was elated when we got an article about our work in the local paper then I was deflated again when I couldn't win our community over at a city council meeting. Each little victory or defeat was all very personal. It was a battlefield where I worked out my hopes and fears. I got a lot of my personal needs met at work, and this made the roller-coaster rides even more intense. But because I was running relatively small programs, I wasn't put in situations where I could be tempted to work around the clock and act out all of my compulsive desires.

At least not until I took an administrative position in a more corporate environment. I can't blame the organization. It was very well run. And my supervisor was an excellent manager and a very nice person. But I took the opportunities as they presented themselves and became the best "passionate workaholic" I could be.

A "passionate workaholic" is someone who meets all the

criteria of being work addicted: She spends most waking moments at work or thinking about work; risks her health, relationships and well-being to work long hours; and doesn't set limits that would keep her stress at a healthy level. A passionate workaholic feels that she's on a mission to save the world from evil, like human rights abuses or drunk drivers. Unfortunately, the passionate workaholic doesn't realize that she's compromising her own future because of her fanatical devotion to the cause. And while garden-variety workaholics may get pressured by spouses or physicians until they realize that they've spent years of avoiding what they care about most in order to work, passionate workaholics feel like the best use of their time *is* furthering their cause. Because they feel like they're on a mission, they feel guilty if they slow down.

At first I was very proud of myself. I took home a bulging brief-case most weekends. I hoped for, and got, more responsibility as time went on. I supervised employees, I ran programs, I met with clients. I had lots of ideas and was generally well liked and re-spected by my peers and supervisor. I was finally a grown-up!

What Do You Mean, I Hate My Job?!

Except . . . I was exhausted most evenings and weekends, so I wasn't much fun to be with. I was very serious and usually think-ing about work or recovering from work. I was a boring worker bee with the delusion that I was doing exactly what I wanted. On vaca-tion during that period, my husband casually commented on the fact that I hated my job. That wasn't even his point. He just took that for granted.

I was shocked. "What do you mean, I hate my job?!"

"You mean you don't know that you hate your job? It's pretty obvious," he said, irritated that he couldn't get to his main point because I wanted to argue about something so self-evident.

Before I could think of how to explain to this deluded man how much I loved my job, I started crying hard like you do when you've been tense for a long time and can finally let your guard down.

My body betrayed me. I wasn't going to convince my husband that I loved my job while I was sniffling, red-eyed and miserable. Back then, I saw these interactions in terms of winning or losing an argument. Like in most courtrooms, there was no search for the Truth. I would make my case using any evidence that supported my point and argue fiercely against any evidence that hurt my stance. (Those were not very productive discussions.)

But that day I was forced to realize that I didn't love my job. No, I haven't been moving ever-steadily forward without setbacks. And I didn't find my career path that day, either. But I did realize that I had been lying to my true self, and that I didn't have a solid foundation to build my life and career on. I am deeply grateful that I was an unsuccessful workaholic.

Not Everyone Is Lucky Enough to Fail at Being a Workaholic

The "passionate workaholic" approach to our career is very attractive to many of us. I tried my best to emulate what seemed from the outside to be the enthusiasm and conviction of other workaholics. Just like most promising addicts, I started out with a positive experience. I felt needed and important, and work filled the free time that I couldn't enjoy without guilt anyway. At first, it seemed like so many problems were solved at once. I found out later about the dark side to what I was doing.

Mine wasn't an extreme case of work obsession. I don't have a war story to top anyone else's. Each of us has our own limit (or bottom), and I'm very thankful I didn't have a more exciting, dramatic story with the obligatory near-death experience or guilt over missing a child's wedding because I had an important client meeting. From the outside, mine is just a run-of-the-mill story of work obsession. But from the inside, I felt like I was a character in a Kafka story. Trapped, confused, trying to do the right thing, yet dead inside.

Only You Can Know
What Your Dark Side Looks Like

I've learned a lot from being a workaholic. I know the trapped, anxious feeling that lets me know that the best part of me isn't the part making the decisions. We all have to face our dark side, whatever that is. It's a little different for everyone. And there's no easy formula for breaking through to the other side. I'll share with you what I believe to be a healthy antidote to the "passionate workaholic" complex. But only you can know what your dark side looks like, how it deceives and takes advantage of your true self and what way of being in the world allows you to stay in touch with and nourish your true self or soul.

I learned that I couldn't survive by my drive and emotional attachment to my work alone. I learned that seeing life as a problem, taking setbacks and advances personally, and imposing my answers on others isn't how I want to live, work or lead others. And I learned that there's a natural flow to what we do in life and how to find and follow it.

Following the Flow of Your Career Path Versus Being Fueled by Emotion

What's wrong with being fueled by emotion? It seems that lots of successful people are fueled by emotion. For some, it's their anger at an injustice. For others, it's a passionate desire to change how something is currently done. And others have had painful childhoods and don't want their children to suffer as they did. There are as many reasons for this as there are people, but the emotionally charged, driven entrepreneur is a familiar presence in magazines, newspapers and television.

Let's first think about what it's like to be fueled by emotion. When you're fueled by emotion, you're volunteering for a roller-coaster ride. When you sign up a new client, you feel elated. Then when you go a few days without a lead, you start to doubt your abilities. But then you get quoted by the local paper. You feel great again. You have lots of adrenaline to use to follow up on all of the leads that resulted from your appearance.

But when the calls slow down, you realize that you're exhausted from all the excitement and work you just did. You figure that the next step is to find some more excitement to give you that elated feeling again. You feel less and less enthused about your work after a few months of toiling away without anything exciting happening. And even the highs get shorter and less thrilling after a couple of years.

Using emotion as a fuel source quickly makes you dependent on it. And when you're locked into the world of emotions, you lose your ability to grow as a person and become wiser. You just get older without any of the perks. And when your emotional fuel burns out, so do you.

When the Adrenaline Runs Dry

Many of the burned-out people I work with started off very excited by their new business or new career. But instead of grounding themselves with a plan based on their values and priorities, or any link to what they find meaningful in life, they were running on adrenaline. Fran started up a restaurant seven years ago. She loved to cook, and her children were in college, and she couldn't have been more sure that this was "meant to be," as she puts it. "At first, I felt like I was living a dream. It was really exciting. I'd look forward to waking up each morning because there would be something fun to do. I'd choose the paint color for the walls, or I'd buy the china for the place settings. I felt like I was playing house. I didn't sleep enough, and I stopped exercising, but I felt energized by making this restaurant happen."

Living off the energy from adrenaline does work, but only for a relatively brief amount of time. After the adrenaline begins to wear off, the first thing that happens is that we get concerned that the fuel source we've depended on is no longer there for us. It's harder to wake up as early. It's harder to push on into the evening and ignore our other interests and responsibilities. The excitement has worn off, and it becomes harder and harder to ignore the day-to-day chores and details of life that have been building up and need attention.

"Everything was going smoothly for a while," remembers Fran. That is until she started feeling bored by some of her restaurant's problems. She assumed she'd be solving interesting problems, like what new recipes to add to the menu, or what toppings would make her wonderful desserts even more wonderful. Instead, she was struggling to find new waitresses and waiters each month, and worrying about whether her bills would get paid on time.

"After a year the thrill, and the energy I got from that thrill, just wasn't there anymore. After the second year I think the only thing that kept me going was fear. I didn't want to be just another failed business. Another restaurant that disappeared." During the third year, Fran used coaching to help her "detox" from her addiction to adrenaline. (I'll discuss the antidote to being a Passionate Workaholic later in this chapter.) She ended up selling the restaurant, which was not the right business for her. Now she's starting up a small catering company, specializing in corporate events. She'll still have staffing and other tedious problems to deal with, but she can control which events she takes on, and her new business allows her to focus more on the creative parts that she loves about her work. Fran explains, "I'm back to having fun with food again and without a lot of the overhead and grind of running a restaurant."

You Can Start to Feel Dead Inside

Many people try to find a substitute for the adrenaline, like caffeine, or more potent drugs in some cases. Some hope that attending a motivational seminar will rekindle their spark. Others find that their fear of failure provides some adrenaline rushes for a while. But, at this point they're close to getting burned out. They're starting to feel dead inside but usually don't recognize this important warning sign. Like a gambler who is sure he or she is just about to go on a winning streak, those suffering career burnout feel that an upcoming big break will erase their problems and show them that their denial of their instincts and feelings is appropriate. This is how the worst cases of burnout get so bad.

It's hard for most people to get *severely* burned out because they become too frustrated to continue their path of self-destruction beyond a certain point. Only those with lots of perseverance and an intolerance of failure can press on until they are dangerously depleted.

If You Can See the Disaster Ahead, You Can Change Your Course

I mentioned that being fueled by adrenaline and excitement eventually leads to relying on fear of failure as an alternate fuel source. Do you have an inner sense that fueling your work with adrenaline and excitement will eventually lead to your relying on other "low-grade" fuel sources? If you can identify this as a likely pathway, you can do a lot to prevent yourself from sliding into the darkness and tunnel vision experience of life that comes with these fuel sources. If you can see that you're on a dangerous path, you may be able to motivate yourself to find a higher-level fuel source that will not exhaust you, but will replenish itself and maintain its intensity over an entire career or even a lifetime.

Finding the natural flow of your career path is like jumping into a river with a raft and learning how to ride the current.

Finding the natural flow of your career path is that higher-level fuel source. In fact, it doesn't look like a fuel source. It's more like jumping into a river with a raft and learning how to ride the current.

When you follow the flow of your career path, you notice what interests you and what draws you in. You feel naturally drawn to explore some areas of interest more than others. But it's with a calm feeling of interest and curiosity, not a manic high that disrupts your feeling grounded.

You neither obsess about, nor avoid, the details of your career path when you're in flow. You don't have a lot of really "high" days nor a lot of horribly "low" days. You do have an inner feeling that what you are doing is a good match for you and that it feels right.

It's Like Falling in Love

Discovering the right career path has quite a bit in common with meeting someone you will eventually fall in love with. You probably wouldn't take a clipboard, go through the phone book and list men's names and numbers, and call each of them with five questions that will help you decide with whom to become intimate. You do what interests you and let friends know that you're available. You meet people along the way. You have a basic understanding of what you're looking for and what you won't put up with. And then you finally feel a spark with someone. So you meet for coffee or talk on the phone. If that spark is still sparking, you have lunch or dinner. You follow your instincts and notice how he treats you. Does he call or show up when he say he will? Is he considerate? Funny? Sweet? Thoughtful? Is that spark still there?

The more desperate you are, and the more you try to control the flow of the relationship, the less likely it will take off on its own. You can really strangle a promising relationship by micromanaging it, and you can nurture a beautiful relationship by allowing it the room to grow. The same goes for your career path.

 Trail Marker: *Think about how you are trying to control the flow of your career path, and how you can let it take on a life of its own.*

Don't Limit Yourself to What You Can Control

Just as you can't predict who you'll fall in love with before you meet them, you can't describe your perfect career before you find it. And if you could describe it, you'd limit yourself to what you *can know* and *can control*. But, you can describe what excites you, what turns you off, what brings out your potential and what allows you the time and energy to have a meaningful personal and family life.

These ideas go against the common wisdom of our culture. We expect ourselves to take the initiative, plan every aspect of our lives and enter those plans into our organizers. Workshops usually tell us how to design, manage and orchestrate our career paths, not how to follow a mysterious flow. And what are we supposed to tell our families and friends when they ask for the update on our careers that is supposed to sound like an application for "Professional of the Year Award?" That we are "going with the flow" and we'll get back to them about where it's going when we find out?

Don't Settle for Being Happy

If by happy we mean a temporary state of mind that feels cheerful or giddy, then it's not worth the price you'll pay to try to maintain it. Happiness is very superficial compared to deeper, more stable states like peace, serenity and a calm inner sense of well-being.

Being happy, sad, giddy, irritated and other superficial feelings are like being tossed around on top of the ocean. There are fewer ups and downs and more stability the deeper you go.

Mihaly Csikszentmihalyi, in his book *Finding Flow*, describes "flow" as ". . . the sense of effortless action [we] feel in moments that stand out as the best in [our] lives."[6]

---

[6] Csikszentmihalyi, Mihaly. *Finding Flow: The Psychology of Engagement with Everyday Life*. New York: Basic Books, 1997. p. 29.

Joseph Campbell puts it this way: "We must be willing to get rid of the life we've planned, so as to have the life that is waiting for us."[7]

Joseph Campbell makes this sound so simple, but how do you begin getting rid of the life you've planned to have the life waiting for you? My experience is that it's easier, but not wiser, to take action than not to take action.

If I get an idea that inspires me, I too often jump up (abandoning whatever else I'm doing, of course) and rush to act on this brainstorm. My adrenaline starts to flow, I start to get excited about the outcome of this new idea, and my peace of mind and patience are instantly devalued. I give myself tunnel vision and lose my focus on my overall life. I get out of touch with my intuition and ability to tolerate frustration. It's as if I just took a drug. I go from mental clarity and a calm inner understanding to rushing around in a big hurry to get something accomplished.

The hardest part was identifying this as a problem. As with so many of my character flaws, I first saw it as a strength. That was my biggest hurdle to addressing this issue. Eventually, I saw that I got distracted, lost my focus and felt driven. I finally admitted that this trait got in my way. Even then, I couldn't always tell when I was losing my grounding as it was happening.

First You Have to Find Your Flow

Robin, now a thirty-three-year-old financial advisor, needed to isolate herself from people who expected her to be the way she'd always been before she made the decision to leave her job as a

---

[7] Osbon, Diane K., Ed. *Reflections on the Art of Living: A Joseph Campbell Companion*. New York: Harper Collins, 1991. p. 18.

corporate attorney. She explained that this was the only way she could turn within, get focused on her inner life and stay focused. "It all hit at once," Robin said. "The transition was negative at first. Kind of like the pupa stage of a butterfly. It's not a miniature butterfly in there waiting to burst out. It's a bunch of icky mush still turning into a butterfly. I literally shut myself down, and shut out anyone who wanted me to stay the person I was. I turned to new people and new situations, and spent a lot of time trying to figure out how to snap out of it. It took a real meltdown to finally do that for me before everything fell into place."

Most of us who make this transition from being an external person to valuing our true self have some period of retreating from our external lives while we regroup, as I mentioned in chapter 1. I think that's why some of our families and friends worry that we'll become isolated and lonely, or even leave them behind. This has some truth to it, but their concern is only partially for our benefit. It's more about their loss of a friend or relative with whom they can gossip or waste time doing meaningless activities, or someone who will validate that their life is not wasted after all. Someone to agree that they are living right.

Their frequent questioning of how our career search is going can be very upsetting to the process. "You can't dig up carrots every day to see how they're doing," my husband says to remind me that I have to tolerate not knowing how things will turn out if I want to make it through the growth process.

When you retreat from the frantic pace of the world around you to find the flow of your life, you disturb the peaceful trance of others who don't appreciate your more vibrant perceptions of yourself, the world around you and them. "Eventually, it became clear and inevitable," Robin described. "I quit pretending to be what I wasn't and started running toward who I really am. I'm afraid some relationships suffered through this transition, but my real friends stuck with me. I learned a lot very quickly about myself and about life, and hung on to what was real for me. It's sure been worth it!"

Non-Doing Can Take More Effort Than Doing

Can you deal with the most vital
matters by letting events take their course?
Can you step back from your own mind
and thus understand all things?

—TAO TE CHING[8]

Living in flow, or the natural rhythm of your life, isn't a sentence to be isolated and lonely. On the contrary, your need for distraction and your desire to live on life's surface is greatly reduced when you live in flow, and you may find that you feel a new sense of freedom that you've only glimpsed for brief moments in the past. There are other aspects to becoming truly free, like reducing your neediness of others and being able to relate to them more genuinely. These are issues that you may need to work on in psychotherapy or in other ways. They won't automatically resolve themselves as you live more in flow. But living in flow does reduce anxiety, so it can reduce the ways you try to control your anxiety, like avoidance of being alone or compulsive eating.

The idea of *not* acting is one of the hardest concepts in this book, because it's so foreign to what we expect to do to improve

---

[8] Mitchell, Stephen, translator. *Tao Te Ching*. New York: Perennial Classics/Harper Collins, 1994. p. 10.

our lives. You may not know what non-action looks like in real life. Picture yourself patiently and calmly observing yourself and your situation and simply knowing what needs to happen next. You would feel unhurried and as if there is barely any effort needed to do what you know needs to be done. It's so obvious that it almost happens by itself. You aren't forcing anything, you're following the flow of your life in the way that has become clear to you because you were quiet enough to listen and still enough to notice. The Tao Te Ching asks, "Do you have the patience to wait til your mud settles and the water is clear? Can you remain unmoving till the right action arises by itself?"[9]

This doesn't mean that you won't feel challenged. But the challenge comes from either struggling to keep yourself still enough to notice the truth about the situation you're facing or from whatever you bring to the situation that makes it challenging. In other words, following the flow of your life is completely different than avoiding or denying something unpleasant in your life.

I'm writing this in Long Island, New York, where I'm visiting my brother-in-law and nephew, and I find myself projecting years into the future and feeling sick with worry and sadness.

My sister KT died in December 2002. She mysteriously developed toxic shock syndrome, and even with immediate and excellent medical care, she died about two weeks later. KT left behind a two-year-old son, Aiden, who was the light of her life, and a wonderful husband of just over three years, Steve.

I find my mind jumping ahead to the moment in the future when Aiden will understand that his mother is dead. I think, "Maybe he'll be five or six when he begins to understand it." I

---

[9] Op cit., p. 15.

argue with myself, "Maybe he'll be closer to seven or eight before he knows what death really is." Mostly I imagine his pain and sadness in that moment when he realizes what happened.

I feel like I'm about to burst into tears and my stomach hurts. Suddenly I notice that not only am I not in the *present* moment, but I'm *years* away from it.

What good can come out of worrying about the distant future? Won't I have to deal with it in that moment? Isn't that the only time I could *possibly* deal with it?

And won't it be different for Aiden than my fears tell me? I believe he'll be sad about discovering that his mother died very tragically, but he barely remembers her now, eight months after her death. I'm confusing my feelings of loss and grief with his, and on top of that, projecting those feelings into the future. I'm also mixing in my devastation of knowing that KT would have done anything to stay here with Aiden and Steve, and my heart-break for Steve, having to raise a toddler without his wife, and while suffering terribly with his grief.

Suddenly Aiden forces me back into the present . . . "Aunt Resrie, come!" In this moment, a smiling boy with curly blond hair wearing overalls and little boy's workboots wants me to come with him and play. A boy with a remarkable father, somehow able to be loving and yet firm with his son, who is raising him to be secure and have an inner strength so that he'll be able to handle whatever difficulty that he faces when the time comes.

I'm now fully back in the present, where I can observe my sadness and anxiety and let them go . . . and go play with Aiden.

Some people are concerned that by *not* acting on their hunches, ideas and simply when they feel the urge to do something, that they are avoiding taking care of something important. I disagree. Too often our actions are more about avoiding anxiety and less about accomplishing what we convince ourselves is important at that moment. If you're typically passive and are concerned you'll avoid reality and rationalize it as "going with the flow," ask yourself if you are talking about the real flow of your life or if you use the term to mean *staying on the existing course*. If you want to avoid deeper reality, you can do that in so many ways. Avoiding taking action is only one, but hiding behind your activities is often the more dangerous tactic. Non-action is *not* the same as avoiding doing the right thing. It is tolerating our anxiety and not *reacting*. And it is acting more wisely when we do act.

Life is mostly gray areas, not black or white. What's interesting about the gray areas is that when you don't have assumptions and when you approach these gray areas from a detached, curious point of view (and don't feel that the outcome is a reflection on you personally), you can more easily identify the answer or at least the right questions to ask.

"We think what is thinkable; not what is 'true,'" [10] points out Guy Claxton in his book *Hare Brain, Tortoise Mind: How Intelligence Increases When You Think Less*. "To tap into the leisurely ways of knowing, one must dare to wait. Knowing emerges from, and is a response to, not-knowing. Learning—the process of coming to know—emerges from uncertainty [11]. . . . Often learning emerges in a more gradual, holistic way, only after a period of casting around for a vague sense of direction, like a

---

[10] Claxton, Guy. *Hare Brain, Tortoise Mind: How Intelligence Increases When You Think Less*. New Jersey: The Ecco Press, 1997. p. 91.
[11] Op cit., p. 6.

pack of hounds that has lost the scent. . . . To undertake this kind of slow learning, one needs to be able to feel comfortable being 'at sea' for a while."[12]

Detours the Flow Can Take

Once you've begun going with the natural flow of your life, it's not always a joyful drift downstream. There are several detours that can interrupt the natural flow.

Not Trusting That There Is a Natural Flow

If you're directing your life, and you stop directing it, won't it spin out of control? Well, if you're truly in control of each and every detail of your life, I guess it could cause some chaos. But are you really in control of as many of those details as you think?

There's an overall path our life could take if we let it, and our actions, or not recognizing that path when we see it, can get in the way of that process. I don't mean that there's one right job for you. There probably isn't one right spouse for you either. Each time we choose a career path, or a spouse, or to have children at a particular time, we choose a particular life. We bring our lives from the general to the particular. So you can have one particular life or another, but if you choose wisely, you keep choosing a particular life for yourself with the potential to allow you to grow and become more your true self.

To choose wisely, you have to be able to notice what is in tune with, or resonates with, your true self. If you're distracted by what

---

[12] Op cit., pp. 8–9.

you think you ought to do or what would make you look good in others' eyes, you won't be able to stay in tune with your true self, and you'll make a choice for the wrong reason. It's possible to make "the right choice for the wrong reason." But if you don't quickly notice that you did the right thing despite yourself and question your ability to judge what's best for you, then you'll soon do what is natural for this state—start making the wrong choices.

If we pan back to the big picture of our life, our choices basically come down to two main options. We can choose to follow what's best for our true self, or we can choose to follow what our superficial self or ego feels it needs. Then, luck, randomness and all the other elements of our undetermined world play their role. Rather than one path, there are many possible "right" paths. And many more wrong paths look right to the part of us that shouldn't be entrusted with such an important decision—our superficial self or ego.

Being "In the Zone" as an Experience of Flow

I'm not exactly a world-class athlete, but I am a big sports fan. I've heard a lot of athletes talk about "being on their game," or "being in the zone" when they are performing to their potential or even beyond it. Coaches, too, realize that there is only so much information you can give a gifted athlete before you take them "out of their game." Barry Melrose, a former coach of the Los Angeles Kings hockey team who is now an ESPN commentator, used to say that his players "needed to just go out there and have fun" when they desperately needed a win.

One day it occurred to me that when coaches or athletes talk about "just having fun out there," they're trying to say that if players think too much or press too hard they won't get into the zone where they effortlessly do exactly what needs to be done at the right moment. (Do you remember the book, *The Inner Game of Tennis?* It was one of the first of many books on the subject of getting in the zone in physical activities.) If you can feel or at least imagine what it means to be physically in the zone, then you're on your way to recognizing what flow feels like in the rest of your life.

Many of us are, understandably, skeptical about what we can't see, feel or otherwise sense directly. It's easy to put the idea of flow into this category. But you can sense it. And you probably have. Sometimes people refer to moments of being in flow as a "peak experience." Think about a time when you felt that all was right with the world, and you were calm and not reacting or anticipating or doing anything else except being in the moment. That way of experiencing the world doesn't have to be limited to a moment every decade or so.

Trail Marker: *You can cultivate the ability to live in flow by practicing going with the natural flow or pace of your life and loosening your grip on the details of your day-to-day activities.*

You Probably Don't Really Know Why You Feel Good

One reason that people don't have as many peak experiences is that they misunderstand why they have them at all. I had a peak experience many years ago while snow skiing. It lasted several hours. I felt exhilarated and joyful. I didn't feel the usual nagging self-consciousness of watching myself act in the world and critiquing those actions. I figured it was because I was skiing, or at least because I was on vacation. Now I see that was a mistake. That point of view would lead me to think that the only way to recapture that joyous feeling would be to go on another expensive vacation. Now I know that I was only capable of achieving that feeling on a vacation because I was not living in flow in my day-to-day life. Years later, once I changed my life to live more in flow, I've had countless peak experiences that don't seem related to what I'm doing at the time. I can be walking out of my office into a beautiful sunny afternoon, or in my office working with a client. I can be walking my dogs, or playing with my friend's eleven-year-old twin girls. I have detached the peak experience from something I am doing. It's always available within me if I can just get out of the way and get in touch with it.

Anxiety and the mistaken belief that you fully control your life can derail getting in flow. But if you know what flow feels like, you can intuitively get yourself to experience it again and again. Especially if you value that experience and are ready to give up feeling in control.

Needing to Be in Control

Even if you value living in flow, and you'd like to give up the need to feel in control of your life, there are still challenges ahead. We want to be in control for understandable conscious and subconscious reasons. We may have grown up in a chaotic home and as adults are still trying to create some stability so we don't feel at the mercy of forces larger than ourselves. Or, we may not trust anyone else to have our best interest in mind, so we begin to believe that we can control more of our lives than is realistic. Or, we may have an "existential dread" that we haven't yet come to terms with. Being mortal, and knowing it, causes all kinds of psychological and emotional reactions. As humans, we have a fundamental drive to make sense of something so apparently absurd and unfathomable as death. So we compensate by imagining a life where we're the focal point and our actions have ultimate significance.

If you can notice that you're working very hard to create the illusion that you're in control of your life in ways that are clearly out of your league, then you're getting very close to being able to give up this myth. Just as cultures create myths based on their circumstances and their understanding of why they exist, so do each of us create personal myths that make us feel that even random events are meaningful. For example, all primitive cultures have ways of making sense of events like diseases that kill large numbers of its members, floods and solar eclipses. And we each have our ways of understanding why we can't leave our current jobs, or why we're occasionally depressed, and other important aspects of our lives that we pull together into a coherent story.

Another problem with needing to feel in control is that this means that you bring an agenda to the relationships and situations in your life. Since you think you're in charge, you're working hard to ensure that things turn out as you think they should. You have a vision of what the outcome should be. This might include job interviews, blind dates or how much sleep your infant needs. Having an agenda about things you can't control gets in the way of paying attention to the real flow and pace of your life and following that flow. It also sets you up for disappointment when life turns out differently than your agenda.

Having an Agenda

One current theory about why Americans spend so much time at work when most of us claim to want more personal and family time is that there are clear goals at our jobs, and our activities at work have a beginning and an end. There are even rewards for doing a good job. Compare that to the more subtle pleasures of playing with a toddler during their two minutes of attention span, or trying to feed a baby who is spitting out more than she's swallowing, and you can begin to see how structure and immediate gratification overpower the more complex, demanding, less glamorous and often thankless tasks of family life.

Another tool we have at work is the agenda. Bringing an agenda to a meeting can help you stay focused on what's important and make sure those things that need to get done do get done. You can also push ahead when attendees start to get distracted by pointing out, "We still need to make a decision about the Douglas account. Then we can move on to how many sandwiches we need for the meeting tomorrow."

Agendas are excellent guides and give you something to check off as you generate nice concrete answers for each numbered item on the page. The problem is that this isn't a whole lot like your real life. And it shares nothing in common with your internal world. There is no agenda that could cover the important questions in life. No checklist. No one right answer that lets you move on to the next concrete question.

When we wish we had an agenda for our internal life, we're wishing for the wrong tool. But we're so comfortable with the agenda that we don't realize that we're asking for the impossible. Relying on an agenda is about as far as you can get from living in flow.

Addiction to Adrenaline

Another detour that can get us out of flow is the addiction to adrenaline. Since I discussed this at length earlier in the chapter, I won't go into detail here. But living an emotional, driven sort of life is in complete opposition to living in flow. Craving adrenaline means that you need certain types of exciting, exhilarating experiences to fuel your activities. Once you have that need, you're not going with the natural flow of your life.

I've already explained that adrenaline is a dangerous fuel source. Now, I'll tell you how it takes you out of the flow of your life. If being in flow feels relatively effortless and as though you have tapped into the natural rhythm of life, adrenaline feels like you want to conquer the world. Flow feels like you are centered and grounded. Adrenaline feels like you want to handle the details of life on a giant checklist even if there is no higher order to it all. Being in flow allows you to calmly consider what you should do next. Adrenaline doesn't give you time to think. There's lots to do, so you'd better stop fooling around and get back to work. And adrenaline does make work feel like work. Flow feels more like you feel when you're playing.

Similar to a drug like cocaine or methamphetamine, adrenaline makes you feel cranky and impatient, and as if no one else but you could do the job right. So it reinforces the feeling that there's a lot of work to do and you'd better get serious about it. If you're used to being fueled by adrenaline, being in flow can be so subtle that it's hard to notice. And it's certainly less compelling. Having the frantic level of activity that adrenaline craves makes flow feel like you aren't doing enough at first. It's very hard to get out of that habit and to change your pace. Many people find it helpful to make a change when they can take some time off and discover the pace that feels comfortable for them without trying to use it in their work until they are more sure of what it should feel like.

Do You Need to Stay Busy?

Many of us passionate workaholics have a compulsion to stay busy. The thought of hours of unstructured time makes us anxious and we quickly fill it up with activities. Or maybe we need to feel that we're accomplishing something concrete every day. What we don't realize is that this level of activity interferes with our accomplishing what really matters to us in the long run. And it definitely interferes with our ability to listen for our calling and act on it once we hear it.

Activity for its own sake can be a symptom of anxiety or depression[13]. It's a way to avoid feelings or to feel in control if you're otherwise overwhelmed. You may have even tried to slow down or simplify your life, but instead of developing a rich internal life, you ended up in the same rut because you unconsciously found a way to safely stay on the surface of your life. Do you need to stay busy? As soon as something drops off your schedule, do you fill in the time with something else? If you're trying to control your anxiety with the structure of lots of activities, you have to stay busy. Once you resolve the anxiety (with psychotherapy, exercise or meditation, for example) you can enjoy having free time. You'll also feel more free to use your time as you wish.

Once you're no longer afraid of your anxiety, and can tolerate it without having to make it go away, you'll have freed yourself from a huge burden. It's critical to get past this issue if you are to consciously choose how you want to spend your time and your life. Severe anxiety usually requires intensive treatment like psychotherapy. However, moderate anxiety can be reduced by meditation, exercise and disciplining yourself to focus on one thing at a time. These ideas are considered in more detail in chapter 7. Once you address the problem of needing to stay busy on a deeper level, you'll be able to benefit from the useful recommendations in the

---

[13] *If you think you may be depressed, take the Depression Self-Test in Appendix A and see your doctor or qualified mental health professional.*

many popular books dealing with the specifics of simplifying your life. There are some titles mentioned in the resource list for this chapter at the end of the book.

Turning Life into a Problem
So You Can "Solve" It

Do you feel that you're alive due to some sort of miraculously complex series of events? Do you marvel at every aspect of your life, even those that seem unpleasant? As you walk outside into the fresh air, are you often filled with a sense of wonder and joyfulness that you are alive right that moment? Or, do you walk out to your car thinking about what you need to get at the store? Then you remember that they're often out of that item. So you figure out how you'll compensate for that. And then you calculate how many minutes you'll have to get from the store to another errand, which has to be done by a certain time. This is what I mean by turning life into a problem.

Life is not in its essence a problem to be solved. If you're a good problem solver, this might be disappointing, since you're used to thinking that you're playing a game you can win. None of us thinks that we have turned our lives into a problem to be solved. We either think that we have certain real problems that need to be addressed, or we believe that we're practical and sensible and that we do what we must to respond to the various dilemmas in our lives.

If you pay attention to the moment that you turn your life into a problem, you may be able to avoid that detour from living in flow. Pay attention to how often you're more focused on relatively unimportant details than you are on the big picture. Or when you feel that you need a specific external event to happen in order to enjoy your life. Then, once you notice this pattern in your day-to-day life, remind yourself that you can't solve an internal problem with an external solution. Finally, turn your attention to the internal reason you feel you need to be "rescued" by outside events, and try to understand that part of you. This will weaken that habit and allow you to spend more time in flow. The journaling exercise on page 63 may help.

Once you experience flow, and can identify the warning signs that you are using adrenaline, you can prevent the detour from flow.

Steps to Getting Back in Flow:

1. Notice that you are out of flow and that you aren't feeling grounded.

2. Remember specific times when you felt grounded, and what it felt like.

3. Remind yourself why you value being in flow.

4. Don't let yourself get even further from flow by excessive worry about it. Instead, wait patiently until it returns.

Each cycle you go through of losing and reentering flow gets easier. You'll be increasingly aware of the subtle feelings involved. And your trust that you'll return to flow increases each time you do.

Once you've become more aware of being in flow, chapter 3 will help you discover whose idea of success you are striving for, and how to find the right wall against which to lean your ladder.

JOURNALING EXERCISE

1. Are you running on adrenaline? Does fear of failure provide a large percentage of your energy? Do you feel driven or compelled to do what you do?

_____

_____

_____

2. Do you feel that you're avoiding something with activity, or simply jumping into action too quickly?

_____

_____

_____

3. What might you be avoiding with your activity?

_____

_____

4. When have you felt that you are in flow, not forcing things but going with what you felt to be the natural course of your life?

_____

_____

_____

5. How can you get into flow more often? What gets in the way of you experiencing flow more often? (This may include overscheduling yourself so you are often rushing, or anticipating the outcome of what you're doing, which prevents you from being completely present in the moment.)

_____

_____

_____

_____

_____

_____

_____

_____

_____

_____

_____

_____

_____

_____

_____

_____

_____

_____

_____

CHAPTER THREE

Type Two:
Good Girls and Rebels—
Are You Climbing
Someone Else's Ladder?

"There is only one success—
to be able to spend your life in your own way."
—CHRISTOPHER MORLEY

In chapter 1, we discussed the metaphor of climbing a ladder your whole life, only to find that it's against the wrong wall. This chapter discusses the tragic result of a fate worse than climbing *your own* ladder leaning against the wrong wall. That is to be climbing *someone else's* ladder that's up against the wrong wall. Those most likely to fall into this trap are both good girls and rebels. Good girls because they are trying to please an influential person or people whose approval they need. This is usually a parent or parents, but can be a special teacher or mentor. Rebels because they are doing the opposite of what would please that influential person or people. Neither are searching their soul for their calling and acting out of their own passionate interest.

They are responding to someone else's needs and desires one way or the other.

It's painful, but at least there's dignity in realizing you chose the wrong career, since you made the decision. Not making that conscious decision robs you of even that small element of freedom.

Let's first consider how smart women make poor choices.

Choosing Too Young

Hannah, a forty-five-year-old wife and mother of two, spent twenty-two years in the entertainment industry before she realized that she didn't belong there.

When Hannah was twenty-three, the entertainment industry seemed glamorous, and it paid well. She didn't mind the frenetic pace or the wasted time in pointless meetings. She wasn't thinking about how she could make a difference in the lives of others, or about having a flexible schedule. She was single and had an exciting career.

At twenty-three her career choice criteria was very different than it is now at forty-five. At forty-five, Hannah wants a career where she is appreciated and a schedule that allows time for family and for herself. She wants to wake up in the morning and look forward to her work day. And she wants time to play the piano.

 Trail Marker: *Choosing a career path before you know who you are means that it may not meet your needs as those needs change and you mature.*

This is a very natural process. We all need to reevaluate our careers as we grow and as living according to our values becomes more important to us. Our ability to understand ourselves and have insight into our behavior and emotions grows as we mature.

Working in show business, for example, may provide enough perks (and star sightings) to make the drudgery and long hours tolerable when we're in our twenties. But as our priorities and values evolve in our thirties and forties, we're less willing to put up with being treated rudely by someone famous as part of our job description.

Our Families Influence Our Careers

I've worked with women who have suffered through years of law school because their parents told them that they ought to be lawyers. I've also worked with women who never went to college because their parents told them that it would be a waste of money, or that they didn't have what it takes to graduate. These are the obvious examples of adult children living out their parents' wishes or avoiding paths their parents didn't feel were right for them.

Other women react to their parents in more subtle ways, intuitively picking up what their parents don't say directly. Or they may be acting on their parents' fears that they never faced head-on, but were passed on, unresolved, to the next generation.

Shelley is a thirty-two-year-old married woman who works too much. She doesn't need all of the money she earns as bank vice-president. Her husband works full time and earns enough to pay all of their basic expenses. She's a caring and conscientious person, but gets so stressed by the end of the week that when she isn't working on the weekend, she's catching up on sleep. Shelley feels guilty that she doesn't spend more time with her husband, but she hasn't been able to cut back at work.

Shelley's parents divorced when she was four, and her mother struggled to pay the rent for most of Shelley's childhood. Shelley learned from her mother, and from her own experience of her father's irresponsibility, that men can't be counted on to provide for their family, and that women have to earn their own living. Her father wasn't able to support his family financially or emotionally, and Shelley generalized his qualities to include all men.

Instead of questioning the wisdom of these lessons during childhood, and Shelley developed a strong drive to earn more money than she needs. As a result, her long workdays interfere with her quality of life and her relationship with her husband. She feels trapped by her exhausting schedule, but also trapped by her fear of struggling as hard as her mother did to provide food and shelter for her family.

Shelley is very bright, but she has a blind spot in this part of her life. Part of her feels that a buffer of money will shield her from her fear, but her efforts to solve the problems of her childhood by earning more as an adult are part of what is keeping her trapped in an unhealthy and unhappy lifestyle.

Trail Marker: *Pay attention to those areas of your life that you don't approach logically. Ask yourself if you're acting on your parents' fears and/or their unfulfilled promises to themselves.*

Life Can Look Full from the Outside but Feel Empty Inside

An important insight for Shelley was to recognize that she had tried her best to be materially successful, but that she was more unhappy than ever. "On the outside, my life probably looked close to perfect; I had a great husband, an impressive job, a nice home, cars . . . all that stuff. But I got to the point where I didn't want to wake up and go through another day. At first, I didn't know why. I knew people that envied me—who wanted what I had. They didn't know how depressed and empty I felt. I knew one more deal or another award wasn't going to make it better. I had no choice but to try to get some answers."

Shelley took three weeks off from work to do some soul searching. "Just leaving work for three weeks was huge," Shelley explains. "I never thought I could take time for myself . . . you know, without it being a working vacation."

Shelley got into psychotherapy at the same time as she started working with me as a coach, and between the two modalities, she discovered that her drive was not based on a love for her work, but was instead based on a fear of relying on her husband. After challenging her false beliefs that started when she was a child, she can now count on her husband to be there for her emotionally. She's even been able to cut back on her hours at work.

Shelley is lucky that her husband still supports this healthy side of her. Many women like Shelley pick a spouse who is emotionally distant, which confirms their fear that they can't count on anyone else to be there for them. Shelley's husband was very frustrated by her work schedule but believed that Shelley was going to be able to work out her problems and be more available. He saw what I noticed when I got to know Shelley . . . that her fears and frantic activity kept the "real" Shelley trapped. And that once she confronted these fears, she could become who she was meant to be.

Are You a Rebel Without Your Own Cause?

You may not be the "Good Girl" who gave up her own dreams to live out her parents' need to have a doctor in the family. Maybe you feel very independent and are proud of the fact that you surprised everyone and followed an impulse to do something exciting or unusual. When your parents dropped hints about wanting grandchildren, you joined the Peace Corps and spent two years in Africa. Or maybe it was no secret that your parents thought you'd make a great kindergarten teacher, so you became a manager in an international accounting firm.

You may have found your calling and successfully avoided the trap of following your family's wishes. But, you may also have gone to the other extreme and rebelled against your parents. Denise, forty-five, swore she'd never be a housewife. She and her brother grew up in a middle class suburb of Delaware in the 1960s. Denise's mother, Marilyn, had always wanted children and left her secretarial job when pregnant with Denise, her first. Marilyn had enjoyed the busy office environment of the glamorous talent agency in which she worked. But she couldn't have been more excited to leave her job and be a full-time wife and mother.

As children, Denise and her younger brother Darren mistakenly thought that their mother had given up a career that was important to her to raise them. The feminist movement was part of the background in the early 1970s, and it colored Denise's point of view that it is unacceptable to give up a career to be a full-time parent and homemaker. "I felt my mother not only gave up some great career she loved, but I thought somehow that her career was a big part of her identity. I think I was actually a little angry at her for giving all that up for a man and for us kids."

Denise left home at eighteen and went straight to work in sales for a large telecommunications company. She spent a lot of time on business trips and was promoted several times over the seven years she spent with that employer.

Looking back at what had quickly become a grind, Denise is

amazed that she had worked so hard at something she didn't enjoy most of the time. "My answer to any frustration I felt, or any self-doubt, was just to work harder. I was like a train on a track—I'd keep trying to go faster and faster, but I never could get off that track. So, I was still on that same track, in fact I was moving even faster to a destination I didn't want to reach."

Denise now sees that she got on that track because she made a career choice by picking anything that didn't remind her of being a housewife. Instead of being pulled *toward* something compelling, she was running *away* from a fear that she didn't fully understand.

Rebelling involves almost as little of your conscious thought as being the good, compliant girl described earlier. The rebel basically does the opposite of what is expected of them. This gives them the feeling that they have individuated from their family, when what they've really done is run away.

Rebels can face more of a challenge than good girls in one way—they have a harder time identifying that they aren't self-directed. Good girls wake up one day and scream, "Oh my God—I'm still trying to please my parents!" Rebels say, "No one's ever told *me* how to live my life!" But if you're a rebel and know it, you have an important advantage—you are probably less afraid to begin your own search since you deeply value thinking for yourself.

> You enter the forest at the darkest point, where there is no path.
> Where there is a way or path, it is someone else's path.
> You are not on your own path.
> If you follow someone else's way, you are not going to realize
>   your potential.[14]

---

[14] Obson, Diane K., editor. *Reflections on the Art of Living: A Joseph Campbell Companion.* New York: Harper Collins, 1991. p. 22.

Fear, Insecurity or Anxiety Can
Influence Our Choice of Goals and Paths

"If I just had an MBA from a prestigious school I could get the kind of job I dream about. But who's going to take me seriously with an associate's degree from a junior college?" Melanie was convinced that she wasn't following her path because she wasn't good enough. She thought that her problem was that she lacked the credentials to follow her childhood dream of being in public relations.

Melanie felt herself drawn to other careers, but was afraid she would be unsuccessful. At some point she decided it was safer to pursue a practical career path that didn't feel as personally or professionally risky. She rationalized this by reminding herself that no one would take her seriously, but this only led her farther from doing what she felt drawn toward. It can be easier to think about what you really want to do as a "dream." That way, you can keep your dream safe from the challenges that reality would pose. But you also keep your dream safe from acting on it and possibly achieving it.

After several months of coaching and soul searching, Melanie discovered that what she really wanted to do with her career was to help underprivileged children believe that they can be successful, no matter how challenging their lives have been so far. The moment she realized that it's important to her to bring hope into young people's lives, she also saw that being unqualified was not the source of her problems. Once Melanie identified her mission (which we'll discuss in chapter 6) she realized that whatever qualifications she'll need are simply details in an interesting adventure. Her insecurity had kept her stuck on what is only one small piece of a larger puzzle. Now Melanie has an entry-level job with an organization that provides educational and social services to blind children and adolescents. "I start my day talking to the children who benefit from my work. I'm not just pushing papers. I'm solving problems that make their lives and their families' lives better."

Trail Marker: *Trust that once you identify your mission, or your purpose in life, the details will fall into place. In fact, figuring out how to put the pieces together becomes an interesting adventure.*

You Can Choose Poorly if You Don't Listen to Your Calling

Carol, forty-four, has been in an unsatisfying but well-paying job for twenty-two years and is now desperate for change. "At one time I wasn't making much money and took this job knowing that I probably wouldn't like it. I thought I could basically numb myself to the negative environment and do anything for money. That's turned out not to be true."

To Carol, money represented security, control and, in some ways, the ability to shut off other people's questions about how she chose to spend her life: where she lives, where and when she goes on vacation, or the car she drives. In our culture, if you earn enough money or achieve a certain amount of fame, you're considered above reproach. Not many people second-guess you. And if anyone does criticize you for your choices, you can reassure yourself that they're envious of your wealth and prestige.

Carol had the opportunity to listen to her calling but didn't do it. For twenty-two years she thought she could compensate by earning a good living and having an expensive lifestyle. Fortunately, she was eventually able to realize where she made the wrong choice, and remember that at one time she did hear an inner voice trying to direct her somewhere more meaningful and interesting.

"It's not easy trying to figure out what I want to be when I grow up at age forty-four!" explains Carol. "But if I take myself back to when I did hear my calling, I believe I can get myself back on track. It's not going to get any easier if I wait even longer."

Whose Idea of Success Are You Striving For?

Success is a loaded word. What images come to mind for you when you think of the word "success"? For many of us, it means something measurable and outside of yourself. What you picture when you hear the word "success" may be far afield from what type of career you would actually enjoy, and find enriching and meaningful.

In other words, if your goal is to be outwardly successful, you set yourself up to fail. If you believe that success is something measurable and external, and you just need to plan how to get there, you are lost. An important step toward living an inwardly mobile life is to either stop using the word altogether, or consider how you can redefine it in a way that allows you to pursue your calling. This may have nothing to do with what you now imagine success to be. And you're not likely to get much encouragement from our popular culture. Or from your family, who although they probably do want you to be happy, have anxiety about your well-being. This means that they may wish for you to be successful in concrete and unfulfilling ways because they believe that if you are outwardly successful they have then done their job.

When Success Feels Like Failure

After following a group of lottery winners, Brickman, Coates and Janoff-Bulman concluded that despite their sudden increase in wealth, the lottery winners' happiness was no different from that of people struck by traumas, such as blindness or paraplegia. That having more money to spend does not necessarily bring about greater subjective well-being has also been documented on a national scale by David G. Myers. His calculations show that although the adjusted value of after-tax personal income in the United States has more than doubled between 1960 and 1990, the percentage of people describing themselves as "very happy" has remained unchanged at 30 percent.[15]

Wishing for material success, with complete confidence that it will make your life worthwhile, and then finding out that once you get there you still have the same problems as before, is devastatingly disappointing. And to add insult to injury, you now no longer have your dream of material success to look forward to.

VH1's *Behind the Music* proves on most weeknights that if you take ambitious young performers and give them lots of money, groupies and power, they describe their lives as hellish and empty by forty-five minutes past the hour.

When you strive for success and it doesn't change anything inside you, it can feel like you've lost your map of how to get through life. These are some of the most difficult cases of burnout I see in my practice.

---

[15]*Brickman P., et al. "Lottery Winners and Accident Victims: Is Happiness Relative?"* Journal of Personality and Social Psychology 36 (1978), and Myers, David G. The Pursuit of Happiness. *New York: Avon, 1993. Quoted in "If We Are So Rich, Why Aren't We Happy?"* Mihaly Csikszentmihalyi. American Psychologist 54 (1999).

But there *is* hope. Next, I'll describe some ways to get off the ultimately disappointing track of aspiring to external success, and I'll give you some tips on how to shift your focus to success on your terms.

Do We Continually Choose a Meaningful Life, or Does It Eventually Become a Habit?

It's both hard and easy to develop habits that lead to your growth and evolution.

The Hard Part

One of the biggest challenges when embarking on your path will be to do so without the understanding and approval of others, including some friends and acquaintances. It can be very frustrating at times and isn't at all romantic like many current authors or the media would have you think. (See chapter 8 for more on getting the support you need as you create your own path.)

The Easy Part

Surprisingly, valuing your evolution as a person more than your material success doesn't have to take a lot of hand wringing or agonizing. In fact, to outsiders it can look pretty boring. Some of the tips that I've learned over the years include:

- Try to stay conscious each day of what matters most to you, for example, a most important value or a top priority. (No, not your top ten priorities!)
- Detaching from the pull of desires: Pay special attention to how you feel *after* you get something you desired.

■ Do you lose some of the excitement almost immediately?

■ Does it join the growing list of things you had to have but no longer care much about? [If it's hard to see this within yourself, can you spot it in your children or others around you? Does your child think that if they get the (fill in the blank with the toy they are fixated on at the moment) that they will never ask for another toy? Of course *you* can see the bigger picture of how that toy will be the latest on the pile of must-have items that no longer hold their interest.]

• Notice how much time you spend on distracting yourself with low-priority activities like watching TV, surfing the Internet or reading (most) magazines. If you admit that you spend too much time distracting yourself with these activities, you'll be able to drop them more easily than if you try to use willpower to force the issue. (It's worth noting that I don't mean that it's always a waste of time to play spider solitaire or surf the net. Your energy ebbs and flows throughout the day and a little mindless activity can help you transition to your next project.)

• Tolerate your anxiety when you can instead of trying to "do something" to make it go away. Anxiety isn't usually a sign that you're on the wrong path. More often, it's a reaction to change or trying something new. By tolerating your anxiety, you prevent your lowest impulses from determining your path.

• Meditate every day for at least ten minutes. (Start with five minutes if that's what it takes to establish it as a daily habit.) This clears your mind of your normal, moment-by-moment thinking and anxiety, and makes room for higher level thoughts and drives. (See page 219 for a meditation exercise. There are resources for learning to meditate in the resources for this chapter at the end of the book.)

- Refer to your journal if you've been keeping one. If not, start keeping a journal in which you record brief notes about what captures your interest when you're reading, watching TV, browsing in a bookstore, etc.
- And finally, don't be too quick to ask others what they think you should do. Unless they have a lot of wisdom, *don't settle for their answers*.

Success on Your Terms

It may seem natural, even patriotic, to aim for material success. And its opposite—avoiding money issues—is a big problem for many people. But according to those who have reached the heights of their lower-level dreams of money, fame and glamour, external success can feel more like a living hell than the paradise we've been promised. When you get to the point that you fully realize that no *external* reward will permanently change you *inside*, you can strive for success as *you* define it.

JOURNALING EXERCISE

1. Where does your motivation for the following activities come from?

Put a check next to the response that best fits you right now.

Career:
- ❏ I'm not working now
- ❏ I work for a paycheck
- ❏ I question my work if I get a negative evaluation from my supervisor (I don't completely respect my supervisor)
- ❏ I question my work if I get a negative evaluation from my supervisor (I really respect my supervisor)
- ❏ I feel a sense of accomplishment from knowing I handled something well that doesn't depend on whether anyone noticed it or acknowledged me

Creative activities (for example, knitting, painting, gardening, drawing, quilting, etc.):
- ❏ I don't have time for creative pursuits
- ❏ I do creative activities because I can earn money from them, or because if I didn't do it, I'd have to pay someone to do it

❑ I do creative activities because people enjoy getting my crafts as gifts, or ask me to make them something
❑ I do creative activities because I get pleasure from seeing people's enjoyment from them
❑ I do creative activities because it is fulfilling and enjoyable just to do them

2. Now go back and highlight the responses you hope to have five years from now.

How many answers did you both check and highlight, indicating that you are where you want to be already?

How many had quite *different* answers, indicating that you're not where you want to be yet?

3. Who do you need validation or approval from?

_____

_____

_____

4. How do you think that needing validation or approval from others is holding you back?

_____

_____

_____

5. When do you enjoy yourself, feel good about your efforts and don't need external validation or approval? How can you bring that self-assured feeling into those areas where you do need approval?

_____

_____

_____

_____

_____

_____

_____

_____

_____

_____

_____

_____

Cultivate the ability to do things because they are inherently rewarding and enjoyable, not because you get recognition for them. For example, if you're curious about something, it's enjoyable to research and learn about that subject. Notice where you are seeking outside validation or approval and try to get in touch with what you get out of the activity.

CHAPTER FOUR

Type Three:
The Toxic Workplace—
Is Your Spark Being
Extinguished at Work?

"When I started here, this was my ideal job,"
explains Shirley, an animated and friendly woman
with brown sparkly eyes. "I guess I'm like that
cliché about the frog. The water started out nice
and comfortable, and each time it got hotter,
I got used to it. Now it's boiling and
I am going to die if I stay in it."

—SHIRLEY,
PARENTING EDUCATION COORDINATOR

Many of the women I spoke to while writing this book took the safe route in their career and lives. They sacrificed satisfaction for stability. Some made the trade-off consciously. Others only realized later the high price they paid for security, and felt confined and disappointed. And some, like Shirley, started out excited about the great opportunity they had found and watched that opportunity get taken from them one piece at a time. At first, they found a way to rationalize the diminishing enjoyment and challenge, but eventually they didn't even want to wake up in the morning to begin another dreary day of the grind their work had become.

I know of a few exceptions, but most employers are simply not concerned about how meaningful your life is. Some enlightened employers offer ways to reduce employee stress. Some may build a workout room, or pay employees to join a gym. But it isn't realistic to expect your employer to care about your well-being. If you assume it's your responsibility to make sure your life is lived well, you'll be much better prepared to address this important issue with your employer when the need arises. Your employer will try to get what he needs from you. It's your responsibility to advocate for your needs.

Employers from Hell: Rare but Dangerous

On the other hand, you *can* expect your employer not to try to make your life miserable. Do you work for someone who is making an effort to reduce the quality of your life? This is an important topic which I can't cover adequately here. If your employer takes pleasure in your suffering and humiliation, get out immediately without unnecessary delay or complaining, and find an interim position as quickly as you can from which to launch your ideal career path. Don't stay in a toxic environment while you're working toward your long-term plan unless you literally need this job to survive. Most women have other options, so don't give up until you've exhausted yours.

One more point about having an employer from hell: *If you've been there for more than a few months, it's critical that you examine how you got there, how you put up with it for the length of time you did and how you can pick up clues about horrible employers in the future and learn from your painful mistake.* I'd say the same thing if you dated or married an abusive man. This isn't the same as not clicking with someone. You've put yourself in danger and didn't trust your instincts that might have warned you. You have some extra work to do before you can trust your judgement again. Now, let's get back to finding out if your spark is being extinguished.

Is Your Spark Being Extinguished?

If you feel that your job is repetitive and mind-numbing, you're at risk of your spark being extinguished. This chapter will help you begin to to figure out if the root of the problem is something you have caused, or if yours really is the job from hell. I'll give you tips on how to try to make things better, and when to know that it's time to leave. Finally, I'll give you my suggestions for leaving gracefully if that's necessary.

In the first chapter I talked about identifying your calling. And in chapters 2 and 3, I described different types of burnout. The first was caused by feeling driven by your need to throw yourself into your work. The second had to do with choosing a career path based on others' expectations of you, or rebelling against those expectations. This chapter is about having your spark extinguished from the *outside*.

Your spark is that part of your inner life that represents the real you. I usually refer to it as your true self or soul. Imagine a spark that could grow into a flame if tended, or which could blow out if not protected. Our true self is fragile so we keep it protected when the environment is not a safe one. But if we keep it protected and apart from the rest of our lives too long, it may fizzle out. And even if it survives, it can't grow. It's important to make a conscious effort to fan that spark and not to let other people or any other outside influences stamp it out while you nurture it, so it will be less fragile and more illuminating.

It's important to begin with the part *you* play in messing up your own life. That's why I left this type of burnout for last. Now that you've considered how you've driven yourself too hard for a good cause, or chosen poorly, or not at all (which you know *is* a choice,) let's talk about how others can try to mess up your life if you let them. And then we'll talk about how to prevent them from having that opportunity.

Step One: Check Yourself First

Before you look for ways your environment is stifling your creativity and self-expression, check to see if there's something that *you're* bringing to your work life that is making you feel trapped and miserable.

Ask yourself how you contributed to your situation, or allowed it to get to the point where you're burned out. (Later in the chapter, I'll go over how to try to change your work environment, and how to leave if necessary.)

Which of these do you relate to?

❏ Were you tempted to take your job by an impressive title, by working for a prestigious company, or because your job is in a glamorous industry?

❏ Did you see the warning signs along the way, but ignored them because you didn't want to lose those perks?

❏ Did you give up looking for a healthy working environment and/or an interesting job to get more job security?

❏ Are you expecting your job to meet many of your personal, social and even spiritual needs (in other words, the need for connection with others and meaning)?

❏ Do you take your job too personally?

Propping Up Your Ego/Ignoring Warning Signs

If you stayed in an unhealthy situation because it propped up your ego, it's time to face the truth. Your insecurity and need to feel special are sabotaging your personal and professional growth. This isn't something that can be cured by finding a different job that will prop up your ego more effectively.

You may need more than coaching or willpower to reverse this tendency. You may need psychotherapy to get to the root of your insecurity and to prevent that part of you from taking the lead when making important career and relationship decisions.

Do you notice this pattern in relationships outside of work? Women who are attracted to men who make them feel special by giving them occasional extravagant gifts, but who treat them poorly on a regular basis, are usually insecure. Sheri, a twenty-seven-year-old executive assistant at an investment firm, vacillates between feeling that she's special and deserving of first-class treatment, and feeling that she's inadequate and unworthy of love. That makes her vulnerable to overvaluing the luxury vacations and expensive gifts her boyfriend occasionally gives her. These perks are concrete ways for Sheri to be reassured that she's special, and they provide a distraction from the fact that she's with someone who doesn't truly recognize her unique gifts and talents. A secure woman, wanting a real relationship with a caring man, would find those gifts and material prizes unnecessary or excessive. Sheri puts up with a lack of genuine caring that a secure woman wouldn't. For a secure woman, the occasional gifts and extraordinary vacations aren't an acceptable substitute for day-to-day kindness and thoughtfulness.

The more you feel a calm sense of acceptance with someone, including yourself, and the less you need special gifts and fancy amenities, the more real a relationship you have. The kind of relationship that nurtures your spark and encourages you to become your true self. This relates to your job, too. Notice when you use the perks and glamorous aspects of your position to shield you from the reality that your job is demoralizing, unpleasant, too intense or just a bad match for who you really are. Once you become aware of how these fringe benefits are keeping you tied to an unhealthy job or workplace, you can start to emotionally pull back from needing that sort of special treatment.

Settling for Security

If you settled for security, ask yourself how secure your situation really is. There are fewer jobs that offer true job security, as companies frequently merge, sell off divisions and restructure in the current financial climate that demands increasing earnings almost every quarter. This kind of unrealistic growth puts management in the position of having to make changes, even when they're not warranted, to satisfy stockholders.

Or maybe you did choose a secure job, but one that you hate. If so, you're paying too high a price for that security. I'll describe using a short-term plan later in this chapter that allows you to have the stability of a good day job without draining your time and creative energy. A job that's burning you out, even if it provides some stability, is *not* a good day job.

Then, in chapter 6, you'll have an opportunity to clarify and spell out your goals and specifics of your new path. The worksheet in chapter 8, "The Path Is the Goal," puts everything together and you'll be on track to get started on your path.

Don't Take It Personally

The remaining questions in the checklist on pages 86 and 87 had to do with trying to get needs met at work that aren't work-related.

I got caught up in this trend myself in the 1990s. I was very involved with an organization that promoted "social responsibility" in business. This didn't only include not polluting the water, or providing humane working conditions. Companies were also expected to provide work that was challenging and meaningful (so far so good), and to provide for many other needs of its employees (this was where things started to get a little weird.)

Many of the recommendations we came up with would still be smart for employers to embrace. Chair massages for tax preparers the week of April 15, discounts at a local gym and flexible benefit plans for employees that cost the employer very little are all great ideas. But what I (and other business writers) have noticed is that at a certain point employees started to see work as a place to get physical, social and even spiritual needs met, like the need for meaning and to live a purposeful life.

Employees had less and less time off to spend with family, at church/temple and volunteering in their communities. They were working very long days, and there were more social events that were considered mandatory after hours. It's this paradigm shift that was dangerous because many workers began to see their employer as the source of getting social and spiritual needs met, instead of their families, places of worship and communities.

I believe that having a career we find meaningful can be very rewarding, but there are other ways to express our creativity and our desire to be useful, productive and integral members of a community.

When you take your work personally, you set yourself up for a multitude of disappointments. Not getting a raise is not simply a (potentially bad) business decision by your boss, it's a personal insult. Getting a transfer to another department isn't based on whether your boss had a need for a position to be filled over there. It feels like your hard work as part of your team has gone unnoticed, and that you are unappreciated. Being overlooked for a promotion doesn't mean that your boss believes that the newly promoted coworker is a better fit, or that she's more comfortable with her. It's a sign that your boss is playing favorites, and the person who got the coveted position is the treasured employee who can do no wrong, while you're conventional and uninspired.

Those of us who are very sensitive are at high risk for taking our jobs too personally, leading us to assume that others' actions and reactions are meant to humiliate, hurt or shut us out. In reality, these are not the most likely reasons for these actions. If we don't search ourselves first before indulging in the assumption that we've been wronged, we'll never know the truth. Once we're committed to discovering others' true motivations, we're released from feeling hurt or slighted.

Step Two:
Change Your Environment, if Possible

❀ *Lord, give me the serenity to accept
the things I cannot change, the courage to
change the things I can, and the wisdom
to know the difference.*

—Serenity Prayer

Once you've gotten some insight into what *you* bring to the problem, it's time to look at what aspects of *your environment* that you can change.

I usually break this down into two elements with my clients:

- Your relationships with others, particularly supervisors, but also colleagues
- Your job description, including your duties, hours, the flexibility of your schedule, where you work and other specifics that make up your job

Change Your Relationships

When we complain about someone, we describe our feelings, not the objective facts. In fact, if we're venting about work to our husband or another close male friend, we may get annoyed when they ask us questions to clarify what actually happened. We may feel that they don't believe us, or aren't taking our side.

But our feelings aren't facts, and recognizing that there is another side of the story is the first step toward identifying what we can change in our relationships, including those at work.

To do this, first we need to completely put aside *our* interests. Then we need to put ourselves inside the heart and mind of the person driving us crazy. What are their concerns? What do they need from us? Their behavior holds all of the clues we'll need to figure out how to resolve our conflict.

A former client, Rhonda, a thirty-two-year-old social worker who creates discharge plans for hospital patients, had a series of misunderstandings with her supervisor, Pam, culminating in her not getting a raise she felt she was entitled to. Pam seemed to favor Rhonda's coworkers. She returned their calls first, went to lunch with several of them on a regular basis and seemed friendlier to them, according to Rhonda. The situation went from unpleasant to unacceptable "when I wasn't given a raise I'd been promised. Pam said it was due to budget constraints, but some of the other social workers got their raise last year after serving two years in the department. When I called to ask about my raise on my two-year anniversary, I was told that there's no money for raises."

Rhonda had plenty of evidence for her side of the story. The phone calls, the lunches and, of course, the raises others got and that she didn't. Rhonda felt that if others knew the facts, they'd also be outraged and empathize with her disappointment.

So why isn't this a cut and dried case of favoritism? And why should Rhonda have to do anything differently?

The Other Side of the Story

My job with Rhonda was to help her see the other side of the story without discounting her feelings. And then to try to figure out her supervisor's motivations. Then we could discover if there was anything that Rhonda could do to improve their relationship.

"What's your supervisor like? What do you think motivates her?"

Rhonda thought for a moment, then replied, "Well, she *is* very cliquish—you know, like a high school girl would be. She's real outgoing, so she's always planning department meetings, lunches . . . different events for us to go to. I'm not really into that, so sometimes I don't go . . . it wasn't anything personal at first. But then I stopped getting invited unless it was a working lunch."

"So she likes to be the center of attention . . . it sounds like she's motivated by a need for people to like her and prop her up."

Rhonda immediately responded, "Yes! You can see her light up when she's given credit for anything that goes well on the unit."

"And have there been other cutbacks at work?"

Rhonda took a moment to answer. "I guess there have been some. Things have been tighter this year . . . we're really discouraged from working overtime, and it seems to take forever to get supplies."

"So it's possible that if your raise came up last year, you would have gotten one, too, right?"

"It's possible. I hadn't thought of it that way."

Reality Is Usually Simpler

When Rhonda started looking at her situation from Pam's point of view, she started to see that Pam felt slighted when Rhonda didn't accept all of her lunch invitations, and simply spent more time with Rhonda's more outgoing colleagues with whom she had more in common. She spoke to them more often, asking them for their feedback, possibly because they praised her decisions and made her feel important. This situation set Rhonda up to feel like there was a personal aspect to her not getting the raise. (Rhonda found out later that there was a policy change, since at that point she was curious to learn what actually happened.)

Some of what Rhonda described sounds like poor management, but it didn't turn out to be a sinister plot of any kind. Rhonda's boss is human and acted like her department was her social circle. And she neglected to announce budget cutbacks, probably because she didn't want to be the bearer of bad news, so she created an opportunity for misunderstandings and hurt feelings.

Tips for Dealing with a Difficult Person at Work

- Learn what your supervisor's real priorities are when she doesn't spell them out or isn't aware of them herself. Rhonda's supervisor, Pam, really *did* care if her lunch invitations were accepted, even though she didn't make it a point to tell Rhonda. Your supervisor may want to give input on all your projects, and feel slighted when you don't ask for feedback. Or your supervisor may wish you were more independent, and only wants you to show her your work when it's near completion. Tune into their personality to learn about these important clues to getting along with them.

- List your supervisor's (or coworker's) good qualities. Try to balance your negative feelings by looking at her as a whole person, not as your nemesis. The above advice about learning what they need from you only works if you see their needs from their point of view. If you're angry or on the defensive, you'll only see what it feels like to be on the receiving end of their demands. You have to put yourself in their shoes to see beyond their demands to what they need. It doesn't mean that their needs and expectations are actually reasonable. I just want you to be able to identify them so you know what you're dealing with.

- Just by releasing your tension based on feeling slighted, the relationship will improve. The relationship won't have as much of an edge to it because you've let go of your resentment.

Don'ts:

- Never compromise your values to get along with someone.
- Once you know what makes them tick, don't use that understanding to manipulate your supervisor (or anyone else).
- Don't stick around if your boss tries to humiliate you, or if (s)he is verbally or emotionally abusive.

Putting the Truth First Avoids Most Power Struggles

When we relate to someone in a position of power, we're more alert to how they use that power over us. If our parents misused their authority over us when we were small and powerless, it's natural that we'll anticipate a reprisal of that unhealthy relationship with our supervisor. Once we get those sensitivities out of the way, and we want to know the *truth* more than we want our *feelings validated,* we'll be able to resolve most relationship issues.

I see many more cases of misunderstandings and poor management leading to employee stress and hurt feelings than I do of truly bad people taking advantage of completely innocent employees. Most of the time, even if you wouldn't pick your boss to be your best friend, a healthy and functional working relationship is possible if at least one of you is conscious of the dynamics between the two of you.

Of course, there really is no way to have a healthy relationship with a small percentage of people. Sometimes you do need to accept that you've done your best with the aspects of the relationship that you can control, and that it's best to leave an unhealthy environment before you're too depleted and beaten down to do so effectively.

Change Your Job Description

I quoted Shirley at the opening of this chapter. She's an outgoing, enthusiastic and very caring thirty-eight-year-old woman whose job used to allow her to express each of these positive qualities.

Shirley's job in a pediatrician's office used to consist of teaching parenting skills to patients' parents, handling phone calls from parents who were anxious about their child's health or behavior, and sending them literature on helpful topics to supplement her advice. This was Shirley's dream job, and she was thrilled to be with such a progressive doctor.

Little by little, though, over a period of over a year, Shirley's job changed. She explains, "If the changes happened overnight, or if my job title and responsibilities were formally changed, I think I would have immediately started looking for another job. But when the doctor's practice where I worked was bought by a large corporation, I was told that my job was secure. So I got used to the changes with the new owners. A little later I was told that I had to cover all of the company's pediatric offices. So I couldn't stay in one place and talk to parents anymore. By that point, all I was doing was processing paperwork, developing materials and driving all over town to put handouts in waiting rooms."

As Shirley's job allowed her less parent contact, Shirley tried to make the most of it. She'd talk to those parents of patients she ran into in the waiting rooms as she dropped off her materials, and offered to send them helpful information if they were having parenting problems.

But just when she felt that things were settling into a new, although hectic, routine, Shirley's assistant left for another position. Shirley was told that there was a hiring freeze and she couldn't replace her. "That's when the paperwork really started piling up. I couldn't pretend that I loved my job anymore. I never got to leave the office, except for quick trips to place materials at the various doctor's offices. I had no parent contact, and nobody else picked up the slack. That made it *really* frustrating, because not only was my job a chore by this point, but I knew how many parents needed the services I couldn't provide anymore.

"I was totally burned out after that. So I took some time to figure out what I wanted to do. I tried business school, but recently I decided to get into a master's program in Marriage and Family Therapy. As soon as I paid off my old student loans, I cut back my hours, so I'm here part-time now. I'm still doing paperwork," she smiles, "but I feel I'm working on something that is making me grow, so I don't feel so stagnant. And I actually like having a part-time job that helps pay the bills but that doesn't require a lot of energy and creativity. Not growing in this position isn't a problem, because I'm getting the stimulation from my new career. I'm happier and more relaxed because I'm not trying to get more satisfaction from this position than I can get. It's a win-win situation, since I know my job inside and out, and I've been here a while, so it's better for my company than if they had to replace me."

It turns out that as frustrating as her job had become, especially in light of the fact that it was so ideal for her initially, it turned out to be a very good "day job." In other words, Shirley can do her job and still have time and energy left over for her family and more creative activities.

Tips on How to Change Your Job Description

- Make the business case for reducing your hours, having a flexible schedule, working from home, etc. Don't feel like you're asking your boss for a favor.
- Think through what job duties make the best use of your talents and interests and think of ways to emphasize those (or include them) as part of your overall role at work.
- Read articles on Web sites like *www.businessknowhow.com* to learn how to make the business case for a better job description that will work for you and your employer.

Step Three: Leave if You Need To

When you've looked at what *you* bring to your problems at work and have tried to have a positive impact on everything you *can* change, and your environment is still unhealthy, it's time to leave. But now you can leave with a clear conscience, knowing that you've used the opportunity as a learning experience, and that you've tried your best to make it work.

Leaving after trying to improve your job duties and work relationships is *not* a failure. But you'll fail yourself if you stay after you know for certain that your workplace is unhealthy.

Spend Time with People
Who Are Doing What They Love

This implies that you should *stop* spending time with people who aren't doing what they love and aren't taking action to make their lives better. And whatever you do, stop hanging out with people who do nothing but complain about how much they hate what they're doing! This is just deadly to your fulfilling your calling. People like this have a gravitational force field of negativity around them. If you are feeling down, there may be a certain "misery loves company" kind of comfort to be found among these types. But once that gets depressing, you'll find yourself sinking further into despair that nothing is going to change in your life.

Please think about who you spend time with and how you feel when you're with them, as well as how you feel after you've spent time with them. Are you *more* motivated to pursue your dreams? Or *less* motivated? Are you inspired? Or discouraged? Hopeful? Or cynical? Consciously decide to spend more time with those who leave you feeling inspired. And do your best to support others as they pursue their dreams.

The Bottom Line

While it's rare to work for someone truly evil, it's not unusual to feel your energy and enthusiasm depleted by your workplace, job duties or your coworkers. Use these journaling questions to help clarify what is wrong with your situation, and what you can do to reignite your spark.

Journaling Exercise

1. What is the most depleting aspect of your workplace?

_____

_____

_____

2. Go back to the checkboxes on pages 86 and 87. Which do you relate to and why?

_____

_____

_____

3. What should you accept about your situation?

_____

_____

_____

4. What have you tried to change? What should you try to change now?

_____

_____

_____

5. What about your situation makes you think you might need to leave, if anything? Is that the healthiest alternative? What are your other options?

_____

_____

_____

CHAPTER FIVE

Type Four: Parenting Burnout

"I don't have a minute to myself. I never feel rested now that I'm a mom," tells Jodie. "And being a New Yorker, I was used to things happening quickly and on my time schedule. That's a thing of the past," Jodie says, laughing at how much has changed in just under two years since she had her son, David.

Full-time working moms really have two full-time careers. Even those who work part time can feel torn between doing their job to the high standards they were used to when a career was their primary focus, and caring for their child, who needs so much from them. Many working moms feel like there's not enough time in the day to do either job well, no less have time for themselves.

Working Mothers and Burnout

I believe that the answer to this dilemma is not simply better time management. Most working moms don't have any fat to trim in their work or homelife schedules. Critical parent-child and marital relationships are already suffering, so tips like making one errand run per week, or buying in bulk and freezing leftovers won't be life-changing advice to a working mom.

Instead, relief from parenting burnout[16] begins with recognizing how her life has gotten out of control. How choices she's made at certain critical points have logically resulted in a lack of satisfaction that profoundly affects the most important aspects of her life.

Many career-oriented moms get a lot of gratification from feeling a high level of control at work that can't be found in intimate relationships, and they assumed that they'd be able to feel similarly in charge of their time and their lives once their baby arrived.

But once their maternity leave is over, if not sooner, they realize that they no longer have anywhere near the amount of control over their lives as they assumed they would. And now they're too exhausted to properly evaluate these mistaken assumptions or to make the necessary corrections. Even if they could determine the cause of their newfound chaos, their old tools won't help them solve the problem.

This chapter will help you understand parenting burnout, and will offer tips and ideas to help women suffering from this condition. At the end of the chapter, I'll briefly discuss three types of mothers at extremely high risk for burnout: single (and single working) mothers, homeschooling mothers and mothers of a special-needs child.

---

[16] *I'll use the term "parenting burnout" to refer to a loss of pleasure or satisfaction in the parent-child relationship, as opposed to work, which was covered in chapters 2, 3 and 4.*

When Workaholics Have Babies

Although David's birth added a new source of stress, Jodie's dilemma is not a new one for her. But she hadn't previously thought of her self-described workaholism as a problem. "I used to start work at 7:30 A.M., and didn't take a lunch break. I worked 'til 9 or 10 at night. I was a workaholic, but I chose to do it. I got energized from working back then."

When Jodie had the "luxury" of being a workaholic, she didn't have to work smart. She could just work hard. "Now as a business owner and mom, I have more responsibility and more work to do, but half the time to get it done. I have to delegate a lot more, and fortunately I have a lot of experience in my field so I can get things done faster."

Jodie's husband, Sam, thought that once Jodie had a baby, she'd settle down a little and spend more time at home with the family. Jodie explains, "My home life is more stressful than before. Sam deserves more attention than I give him. He works from home, and takes a lot of time off, and I'm not there to spend it with him. I've just told my business partner that I'm going to start working from home three days a week, and that I'll be cutting back to part time in a couple of months. I can't wait to enjoy my family again!"

Any working parent is at risk for parenting burnout. But those who were headed for career burnout before getting pregnant are at much higher risk because their approach to work and life already wasn't working. Add more stress, more responsibility, subtract sleep and you have a recipe for burnout.

It's also hard to get a great deal of meaning out of activities that are done frenetically, no matter how much you love doing them when you have the time to perform them consciously.

Let's say you love to travel. When you dream of going to Paris, Venice, or maybe traveling across the United States, you probably picture walking the streets, eating in charming restaurants and staying in lovely inns. But ask a frequent flyer who's constantly on the road how romantic her travel is. She'll tell you she longs for a home-cooked meal, her own bed and to read to her child before he goes to sleep.

That's what it's like to have both a full-time career you enjoy and a child you love. They're both great, but you don't have the leisure to enjoy either. There are meals to cook, laundry piling up and carpools to drive. In addition, many working moms report that when they finally get a moment to spend with their babies, they find themselves thinking about work. And at work, they're thinking about their baby.

Approaching Parenting Like Another Career

One of the ways that career moms get off track is that they use external rewards, accomplishments and feedback to gauge how successful they are. This is perfectly normal. For example, most people feel that if they earn more money this year than last year, they're more successful. Their friends and family typically agree, which is part of the problem.

We live in a culture that rewards external achievement as success. We can't blame the culture for this. Capitalism both creates a system in which monetary success is a concrete measure of progress, and simultaneously allows individuals freedom unheard of in any other system of government. Even the freedom to value a less materialistic life.

However, when our individual values conform to those in our

external culture, pretty soon we're measuring our success based on our bank account, the car we drive and which parties we get invited to. That's quite a shallow way to critique your worth as a human being.

Inwardly Mobile Women Look in the Right Direction for Self-Fulfillment

The upwardly mobile woman is turned toward the external world for validation, happiness and the satisfaction of all of her needs. But her *essential* needs are not those of her ego, which is what the outside world is geared toward addressing. As she turns inward, it becomes more and more apparent that there's no true satisfaction of her most important needs to be found outside herself.

In chapter 1, I mentioned that unlike the external focus of being upwardly mobile, inward mobility is the process of getting in touch with your calling and listening to your intuition. In order to describe a higher versus a lower form of inner communication, I use the terms "intuition" and "gut feeling" in an idiosyncratic way. I use the term "intuition" to mean an inner voice connected with your soul, and therefore connected to the Divine. I differentiate that from a "gut feeling," which I use to describe a lower form of communication that originates in our primitive mind.

Let's say you're pregnant and you have a hunch that you're carrying a boy. I would call that a "gut feeling," assuming you aren't really able to predict your baby's sex.

On the other hand, you overhear your neighbor hitting and screaming at her young child. Your "gut feeling" tells you that you really shouldn't do something that would make your relationship with your neighbor feel uncomfortable. But when you quiet your mind and consult your "intuition," you hear your inner voice give you direction from a higher vantage point than the part of you that would feel socially awkward. It tells you, "You need to do something to help that girl!"

"Saint Augustine insisted that 'our whole business in this life is to restore to health the eye of the heart whereby God may be seen.' . . . The power of 'The Eye of the Heart,' which produces *insight*, is vastly superior to the power of thought, which produces *opinions*." [17]

Inward Mobility Keeps Our Focus on a Higher Level

It's hard to find communion with the Divine while changing a dirty diaper. But when we *don't* try to connect our day-to-day activities with something higher, we feel like underpaid and overworked maids, nannies and chauffeurs. The inwardly mobile woman is seeking something *higher* than mere ego satisfaction.

"The higher the Level of Being, the greater, richer, and more wonderful is the world."[18]

---

[17] Schumacher, E.F. *A Guide for the Perplexed*. New York: Harper & Row, 1977. p. 47.
[18] Op cit. p. 35.

E-mail from Julie

Subj: Career Coaching
From: julie@bigcompany.com

Dear Leslie:

I read one of your articles about career transition online and was hoping you could give me some suggestions.

I've been in marketing for 11 years and have put up with a lot at my current job thinking it would pay off. Well it hasn't. I just went in for my review and my boss gave me a mediocre review and a minimal raise.

I have a four-year-old son and my husband travels quite a bit. I think it's time to reassess my priorities and spend more time with my son and husband. But I have no idea how to find a satisfying job that allows me time and energy for my family. And it would be great to have a little time for myself at some point!

I've thought about doing career counseling (believe it or not). I've actually been doing this for friends and coworkers informally. I think I'd be good at this but I don't know how to get started. With an Ivy League MBA, strong communication skills, intelligence and insight, I should feel optimistic and full of confidence. But instead I feel defeated by a dead-end job and unsure of what to do next.

Thanks for any help,
Julie

Subj: Re: Career Coaching
From: lesliegodwin@earthlink.net

Dear Julie:

Once you reduce your priorities to just a couple (parenting and personal growth, for example) then you can work on making those priorities more meaningful and rewarding. If you have a career, family, personal life, extended family, and other responsibilities, you can't really do all of them to your level of satisfaction, and you give up depth for breadth.

The defeated feeling you mentioned may be exhaustion, or it may be that you aren't doing what you're supposed to be doing in life. Or a combination.

Can you take a couple of days off to get some perspective on your situation? Day-to-day survival doesn't let you look at the big picture, which is the only way to see where the day-to-day fits in. If you're just surviving, that isn't fulfilling. If your day-to-day is spent on what you most care about and working toward goals and priorities that allow you to know yourself better and express your gifts, you'll probably feel more fulfilled and that you are spending your time wisely.

> Having a young child requires a great deal of
> sacrifice of personal goals for a long time, yet can
> be incredibly meaningful and fulfilling in other ways.
> Be realistic about this while you're struggling with
> these challenges.
>
> Take care,
> Leslie

Julie had a values conflict. She believed and felt that her family comes first. But she spent much more time at work than with her husband or son. And her job had become less rewarding then it used to be. She still enjoyed the break it gave her from the intensity of being a mom and the contact with other adults, and she and Roger depended on her paycheck. But she couldn't deny that sometimes she felt that work took time she wanted to spend playing with four-year-old son, Mark, having adult conversation with Roger, and on her hobby of baking bread. And it would be ideal to have some time to contemplate some of the important changes she was going through.

Experiencing Flow as a Parent

In chapter 2 we discussed how getting into "flow"—those moments when our hearts, minds and will are in harmony—is an antidote to feeling "driven." Athletes call this, "being in the zone." Parents can get in the zone, too. Cultivating attention on the present moment, and being in flow, can illuminate a parent's experience of being with their child. This experience helps the child stay in the present moment, as well. (Children are able to be in the present moment naturally, but when adults don't let them lose themselves in play, or are very anxious, a child can "forget" how to be in flow.)

"Parenting is supposed to be one of the most rewarding experiences in life, but it isn't unless one approaches it with the same attention as one would a sport or an artistic performance. In a study of flow in motherhood, Maria Allison and Margaret Carlisle Duncan described several examples of how the psychic energy invested in a child's growth can produce enjoyment in parenting. Here a mother describes the times she achieves flow: '. . . when I'm working with my daughter; when she's discovering something new. A new cookie recipe that she has accomplished, that she has made herself, an artistic work that she has done that she's proud of. Her reading is one thing that she's really into, and we read together. She reads to me, and I read to her, and that's a time when I sort of lose *touch with the rest of the world, I'm totally absorbed in what I'm doing.* . . . [my emphasis].'

"To experience such simple pleasures of parenting, one has to pay attention to them, to know what the child is 'proud of,' what she is 'into'; then one has to devote more attention to sharing those activities with her."[19]

---

[19] Csikszentmihalyi, Mihaly. *Finding Flow: The Psychology of Engagement with Everyday Life.* New York: Basic Books, 1997. p. 112.

Tips for Getting in Flow with your Child(ren)
Margaret Carlisle Duncan

- **Do things that you particularly enjoy or think you might enjoy with your kids.** Such activities hold a strong potential for flow.

- **Try activities where you and your children are novices together and start at the same level.** It's fun to step out of your role as an expert or authority figure and into the role of student. And you may learn something new about your children and yourself. (For example, when my daughters were eleven and thirteen years old, and I was in my forties, all three of us signed up for a Black Belt program in the martial art of Tae Kwon Do. We went to classes together, tested for our belts together, and participated in tournaments together. We even practiced breaking boards together. For four years we spent "quality time" together and enjoyed talking about Tae Kwon Do—even on those days when we didn't attend class. Our participation in Tae Kwon Do led to family flow experiences.)

- **Select activities that challenge both you and your children.** Make sure your goals are realistic, and your skills match the challenges. The activity should be neither too easy nor too difficult. If it's too easy, you may become bored. If it's too difficult, you may become discouraged. An activity where each of you can progress at your own pace is ideal.

- **Choose experiences that offer you and your children clear goals and immediate feedback.** Sports, games, and competitions are good examples. You know what you're trying to achieve and you know how well you're doing—

with virtually no delay. Whether you're playing Monopoly or tennis, you see the results almost instantaneously. Children, in particular, are less likely to remain interested in activities where feedback is uncertain or delayed.

• **Clear the deck of interruptions and distractions.** Make sure you set aside special time when you and your children can focus on each other. Your resolution not to be interrupted allows you and your kids to concentrate on the experience. (For example, every evening after dinner we used to read the Laura Ingalls Wilder books aloud to each other. I unplugged the phone and the TV. The girls' friends were told that 7:00 to 7:45 P.M. was "sacred" time.)

Child-Centered Parenting

Parenting isn't something to be squeezed into the moments between meetings and meal preparation. Children have irreducible needs, and while these needs vary based on different developmental stages, they're all very time-consuming to meet adequately.

We're not talking about being a perfect parent. D.W. Winnicott, a brilliant pediatrician and groundbreaking psychoanalyst, wrote about "good enough parenting." In other words, no parent could or should protect their child from every frustration. But parents can and should protect them from those feelings, fears and actual dangers that would overwhelm the baby's fragile coping abilities.

I use the term "child-centered parenting" to refer to the starting point of parenting rather than any one parenting technique. The basic idea is that you start with what your child needs. There are different ways to learn about these needs. One of the best is one you're no doubt familiar with: mother's intuition. The way you learned which cry was for a bottle, and which was for a clean diaper. And which was for a walk around the room while being serenaded by a song.

There are books written by experts like Penelope Leach, William Sears and T. Berry Brazelton that help put what your child needs at any given moment into the context of the range of childhood developmental issues, as well as how these relate to adult characteristics. (My favorite is *Your Baby and Child* by Penelope Leach. Other titles are included in the resources for this chapter at the end of the book.) The ones that explain how to get your child to sleep in his own bed in one weekend, or how to get him to use a potty in five hours, are probably not child-centered.

Once the basics are understood, most parents find that they respond intuitively to those needs, incorporating their values, beliefs, and their personality style naturally. Occasionally, it can be helpful to hear what another mom is doing, or to get feedback from your own parents, but most parenting confusion is the result of not fully understanding what your child is going through, combined with a mixture of parental expectations, fears, anxieties and frustrations.

Approaching parenting based on responding to your child's basic needs can help with the job of adjusting your priorities. When you look at parenting from the perspective of what tasks you have to do, what time you have to be at work and which out-of-town clients need some face-time, you mentally develop the equivalent of a giant to-do list. Each item is ranked by priority, usually by how urgent it is, not by how important it is.

When you look at parenting from the perspective of what your child needs, what developmental stage he's in, and what the consequences are to his sense of self if those basic needs aren't met, your to-do list will be ranked by how important each item is for your child, not by external deadlines, or what time your boss expects everyone in to work. Somehow you find a way to spend time with your baby when he's crying because his new tooth is coming in. Or when he just had a bad dream and needs his mommy. The same way you found time to meet your husband for dinner when you started dating, even though you had an important meeting the next day.

Whatever you really value has a very good chance of getting done. Other items will fall down a little farther on the list.

Once you know what your child needs, and why those needs are important, you'll find a way to respond. What he *wants*, of course, is a different story. Child-centered does not mean self-centered.

My Turning Point

Jennifer Johnson
(founder and principal of Johnson & Company, The Virtual Agency™)

"My husband was working in international marketing and was often gone ten to twelve days at a time. I was working at the "dream job" that had finally come my way, and I had the opportunity to go to New York to conduct some focus groups. My husband was flying in from Japan the same night I was leaving, so we planned to meet at the airport and exchange the kids.

"I remember balancing the kids and luggage on an airport cart and racing to his gate, only to find out his flight had been delayed. I was frantic. When his flight finally came in, I literally threw him the kids and raced to my terminal, just barely making my flight.

"I collapsed in my seat, and in a moment of clarity heard something within me say, 'You can't do this. You need to quit your job.'

"I was absolutely giddy. I pulled out a piece of paper and wrote my resignation letter right then.

"I had literally been going crazy over how much of my time was being wasted commuting. That feeling immediately went away when I quit. I had everything I wanted out of a career, but I was shortchanging the things that were really important in my life. I needed to reprioritize and let the most important things drive my decisions, not money or anything else."

In Jennifer's story above, she realized that after she stopped reprioritizing, she found a way to not only do interesting work on a flexible schedule, but to help others do the same. She started Johnson & Company, a public relations and marketing firm, which hires other top-notch experts who want to work flexible schedules, and pools them together to get the job done without the grind of hectic deadlines this field is known for. "I can't imagine ever going back to a corporate job," Jennifer says. "I have no dress code now. I have so much freedom and flexibility that I can't imagine exchanging that."

Making Working Work

"I grew up a latchkey kid until sixth grade," tells Kristine, a working mother of two girls, three-year-old Paige and six-month-old Elizabeth. "My mom was a nurse and dropped me off at day care in the morning, and picked me up in the evening. When I was old enough, I wore a key around my neck, and let myself in the house after school. I wasn't allowed to have friends over since my parents weren't there. I always thought it was so cool that my friends had their mom at home when they got home from school."

Kristine and Joe both worked full time before their first baby was born. But from the beginning, they planned to do things differently than when Kristine was growing up. Since Kristine earned more money at her job as director of promotions for a media firm outside Los Angeles, Joe agreed to see if he could handle staying home with their firstborn, Paige.

"I had three months of maternity leave, then for three months we had a team of family and friends that took care of Paige. We had five people lined up, so no one felt too burdened with babysitting. My parents took her, Joe's parents, and a couple of friends. Then when Paige was six months old, Joe quit his job. We said that if he didn't enjoy taking care of her, we'd figure out a way for me to stay home. But it's been great."

In many ways, Joe and Kristine are a traditional family. They're active in their church and their families live close by and are involved with their grandchildren. But this unusual arrangement really suits each of their personalities. Kristine is more ambitious than Joe. And Joe enjoys doing chores and fix-it projects around the house.

Kristine is still "mommy," and Joe is definitely the dad. He takes Paige bowling and lizard hunting. She's even become a NASCAR fan from watching races on TV with her dad. But there are times when Paige will wake up in the middle of the night and call out for daddy.

Kristine's Tips for Working Moms

• Pinch pennies. Reduce your financial stress by being as frugal as possible.

• Don't worry about what other couples are buying, or vacations they are taking.

Kristine says, "I've always been cheap. They call me 'Penny' at work. We spent more before the kids, but never had an extravagant lifestyle. We went to marital counseling at church before we got married. Our minister explained how a family can live on one salary. I recommend that kind of premarital meeting with their clergyperson to other couples.

"One of my friends is a stay-at-home mom and her husband works full time. They're still renting, they buy name brands and he's not handy around the house. I worry about them digging themselves deeper into debt."

Trail Marker: *Don't compare your lifestyle to anyone else's. As they say in 12-step programs, "Don't compare your insides with anyone else's outsides."*

Paige and Elizabeth have the stability of having their dad around most of the time, and their mom is home a lot. But simply working at home doesn't mean you're a stay-at-home parent. Without another parent handling child care, you'd need to hire someone to care for your child while you're working. It means a lot to Paige to see her mom around the house so much, and Elizabeth gets breast-fed those days that Kristine is home. But the success of this method hinges on Joe being available to care for the children. And his willingness to be a stay-at-home dad.

Stay-at-Home Moms Get
Burned Out, Too

"By the end of summer, I couldn't stand one more argument between the girls," tells Carrie, a stay-at-home mother of twin eleven-year-old daughters. "I got so tired of thinking of creative ways to get them to stop fighting. We just saw too much of each other. When they're in school, I look forward to seeing them when they get home."

Working moms have some advantages over stay-at-home moms: knowing they can get through their (job-related) to-do list for the day, hearing that they look nice or that they did a good job on a project and spending hours wearing something stylish that's not covered in juice or baby food or colored with a marker.

Stay-at-home moms don't have the variety of tasks, have few people to talk to about adult subjects and don't get the same short-term feeling of accomplishment from the less-than-instant gratification of raising children and caring for a home and husband that helps working moms maintain their adult identity.

"I have no control over my time like I did before I had kids," explains Carrie. "For example, a simple thing like reading the paper while I'm eating my breakfast. The girls talk a mile a minute at the breakfast table . . . about what they dreamed last night, what someone said last year at school, or what new outfit they want Grandma to get for their American Girl doll. I can't concentrate long enough to read even one section of the paper."

It is easy to feel like you're doing chores, not raising a family. Or that you're doing laundry, cooking and cleaning, and not being a loving and caring wife. And being too tired to dress up and enjoy adult company and grown-up entertainment means that you can feel that you're no longer a cherished wife and best friend.

Being a stay-at-home mom reduces the conflicting pressures of balancing stress at work and all the duties of caring for a home and family. But it doesn't necessarily make it any more likely that a stay-at-home mom will feel that her life is meaningful. Unless she's an inwardly mobile stay-at-home mom.

The Inwardly Mobile Stay-at-Home Mom

Meaning is not something earned from a job well-done, by the brand of SUV parked in the driveway or your child's grade point average. Meaning is based on the depth of the connection between the way you spend your life and who you are in your essence or soul.

Most of us assume that we're spending our lives moving toward our dreams and aspirations. But if you think about how you spend each day, *that* is actually how you're spending your life.

Being a full-time parent can easily feel like being an unpaid nurse, nanny, maid, cook and sleep-deprivation-experiment

Meaning is based on the depth of the connection between the way you spend your life and who you are in your essence or soul.

subject all rolled into one unappreciated human being. On the other hand, consciously parenting may be the most meaningful thing you can possibly do. It's probably the most important.

The Missing Tile

When you're around your children most of the time, it's easy to lose the sense of wonder you had when they were born, and simply focus on the crisis of the moment. Dennis Prager, in his book, *Happiness Is a Serious Problem*, explains his "Theory of the Missing Tile." "One of human nature's most effective ways of sabotaging happiness is to look at a beautiful scene and fixate on whatever is flawed or missing, no matter how small. This tendency is easily demonstrated. Imagine looking up at a tiled ceiling from which one tile is missing—you will most likely concentrate on that missing tile. In fact, the more beautiful the ceiling, the more you are likely to concentrate on the missing tile and permit it to affect your enjoyment of the rest of the ceiling." [20]

Similarly, we can easily overlook many of the positive and interesting things our children do and say, while the occasional mistake stands out and gets our attention. This is true in any relationship, including the way we see ourselves. I've even noticed this when I'm training my Great Danes, Finn (a black Dane from a local rescue) and Savannah (a Harlequin Dane who came to us as a foster and stayed).

At first, I noticed what they did wrong and told them to stop it. Then, I noticed when they stopped what they were doing, and I praised them for not being bad. Now, I notice (and reward them) when they spontaneously do the right thing.

It surprised my husband, Bob, the first time he heard me praise Finn for lying quietly in the living room.

---

[20] Prager, Dennis. *Happiness Is a Serious Problem: A Human Nature Repair Manual*. New York: Regan Books, 1999. p. 31.

"What do you mean, 'Good boy?' He didn't do anything?!"

"He's being good, lying there so nicely," I explained. "He's providing dog ambiance and he's not bothering us, or chasing the cat or barking."

Now I really notice when he's being good and tell him I appreciate it. It's made a big difference in his behavior. I've even overheard my husband say "Good quiet boy!" when Finn stops barking.

Trail Marker: *Catch your child doing something good. It'll make him feel like you notice that he's a good person, too, not just a flawed boy who needs your guidance.*

Children Are a Blessing

"It's easy for me to take my girls for granted now," Carrie says. "But we tried for three years to have children before I got pregnant. Then when I finally did get pregnant, I had to be on bedrest for months. For the first year of their lives, every time I went to church, I felt so grateful to have them, I burst into tears."

A critical part of conscious parenting, and being in flow, is being present in the moment. Having children is a lot of work. It's also a tremendous psychological burden to have helpless, but very active, little people who are so dependent on you. Think about how you can stay in the moment, not get lost in what you have to do hours from now, and how you can avoid letting your anxiety push you up to the surface of your life.

Susie Michelle Cortright, in her book *More Energy Now!*, recommends we:

> . . . *decide which tasks (and people) deserve your full attention. Then give it. As you do so, work on full-sensory awareness. What does your child's hair smell like? How does she look at you? How does her hand feel in yours? What will you remember about this moment for years to come?*
>
> *Think about how much better it is to slow down, to get lost in the moment, to appreciate every one of our God-given, miraculous moments by creating an environment of serenity, peace, and pure productivity. A place where there is no frantic, frenzied rushing but only a singular focus that guides us to the next task and the next, throughout the day.*
>
> *Your life is made up of ordinary moments, and it's foolish to rush them in an attempt to find a bigger, better, more dramatic moment. Joy exists in the mundane tasks, and learning to immerse yourself in them brings a quiet, powerful form of energy.*[21]

---

[21] Cortright, Susie Michelle. *More Energy Now! How to Beat Mommy Burnout and Live with Vitality, Passion, and Joy.* Excerpt found on: http://www.kinderstart.com:8080/kindertoday/ 995192941/index_html

Carrie's Tips for Moms:

- **Put yourself in different settings, like the beach, church, even furniture shopping.** My girls act differently in different places or when we're doing something new, so even though I'm with the same kids, I don't feel we're in a rut.

- **Let your kids pursue what they love to do.** Mine love animals, so we occasionally visit the cat condos at the local shelter, we foster kittens during summer vacation and we take one of our dogs to agility classes.

- **Get help for short periods of time from people you trust.** My neighbor loves kids, but doesn't have any of her own. Every week she borrows my girls and they play at her house or go on an outing. She loves being part of our extended family and having a close relationship with the girls, and I get half a day or more to get some work done, or go on a date with my husband without paying for a baby-sitter.

Conscious parenting by an inwardly mobile mother has rich rewards, because she can see her child thriving in ways that upwardly mobile parents, focused on the external, visible achievements of their child, will miss. An inwardly mobile mother understands herself, knows the difference between what gratifies her ego and what nourishes her soul. She can then apply this wisdom to mothering. She can recognize the souls of her children and speak to that Divine part of them, drawing them out and encouraging them to recognize that they're infinitely valuable because of what is inside of them. It's harder to do this when her three-year-old has just knocked over the milk carton and milk is pouring onto the report she's been working on for months. Or when her baby throws up on her mother-in-law's lap. But the inwardly mobile mom can regroup more quickly after these disasters and rediscover the Divine part within herself and her children.

Carrie's twin girls fostered kittens again this year as a summer project. Carrie had a feeling that this activity would teach them lessons that a lecture could never accomplish. The local shelter needs foster homes for their very young kittens who can't yet be adopted out, since they're still nursing on their mother. This summer they fostered two, three-week-old kittens for five weeks.

"When I saw how responsible and diligent the girls were about doing all the kitten care—the feeding, the poop-scooping, the playing—even when they didn't feel like it, I realized I had raised some really wonderful people. It was worth it to have spent so much time with them, since it's resulted in kids who have empathy for other creatures, and the discipline to follow through with hard work. I'm so proud of them!"

Other High-Risk Situations
for Parenting Burnout

If I stop and think about what
I have to do each day, I'd be paralyzed.
I don't know how I do it. But I put my kids'
well-being first, then everything else has
to fit into my life, including my job.

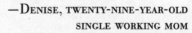

—Denise, twenty-nine-year-old
single working mom

Single Working Moms/Single Moms

If you're a single mother[22] who wants to live an inwardly mobile life, you don't have the luxury of losing focus on this goal. While the rest of us can get distracted once in a while, or fall into bad habits, you have to be intensely focused on your goal of paying attention to your inner life or else fall prey to the chaos of your outer life. This can be a blessing in disguise, but it's also incredibly hard to be so disciplined.

The most obvious difficulty that you face as a single mother is that you don't have a husband to share the adult aspects of life. You probably don't have someone to lie in bed with and talk through your concerns about house rules or discipline questions, or to simply share the joy of having a wonderful child. And if something needs to get done, it's probably you who will do it. There's little division of labor, except for the household chores that your kids are able to do.

Single Moms Don't Have Time to Wander Off Their Path

If you're going to dedicate yourself to an inwardly mobile life, and you have the challenges of being a single mom, you'll have to stay intensely focused on your path. There will be continual distractions and disruptions. People, places and things will try to take you away from your calm center and get you excited, disappointed, fearful, anxious and frazzled. Reverend Sandra Yarlott,

---

[22] I'll use the term "single mother" as a shortcut to include divorced mothers, those who have never been married and widowed mothers, for the sake of brevity. Each of those reasons for being currently unmarried carries different elements that make it quite different from the others, so I'm leaving out some important information by grouping them together.

Director of the Spiritual Care Program at UCLA Medical Center in Los Angeles, comments on developing the ability to stay calm when there's chaos around you. "I liken it to the image of the eye of the tornado. The tornado is a terrifying whirlwind power. But in the center of it is absolute silence. So how do you stand in that silence in the midst of your children, and your phone's ringing, and you're late for an appointment, and whatever else are the demands of your work?"

Reverend Yarlott points out that when you have a practice like meditation or contemplation (she calls it sitting in silence), you find a deep place within yourself that you can't find any other way. She says, "when you sit in silence, you notice there is something deeper than the fear, deeper than the anxiety. There is a silence underneath that. You develop an inner observer, and it's part of your self but it doesn't judge, doesn't get hooked into emotions or thoughts. It can just say, 'Oh that's fear' and observe it and come back to the quiet, 'Oh future planning,' observe it and come back to the quiet.

"It's a discipline. A strong emotion comes up and all our energy and attention hooks into that emotion. But there's a space inside of us where we can observe ourselves and come back to the calm place without merging with the emotion."

How Can You Find That Calm Place?

If you want to live a meaningful life, not just a productive life, you need to deepen yourself. There are many ways to do this, but it's probably the hardest single thing to cultivate, especially without a lot of free time and energy. But at the same time, what's the alternative? To live on the surface of life, focusing on doing and not being? Or just waiting until you have more time in that fictitious "someday" that may or may not come?

Why not live every day purposefully and model that attitude and discipline for your children? A single working mother of three, Anita, has been seeing me for psychotherapy for several years. When she started out, she was frequently overwhelmed. She was overwhelmed by her irresponsible ex-husband, who never made a child-support payment without being nagged, and even then, skipped years without paying. She was overwhelmed by her mother, who was very distant and cold, making Anita feel like she was never good enough. And she was overwhelmed by how needy her own three children seemed. Or maybe it just seemed that they were incredibly needy after a day in a very demanding job as a family law attorney, and she couldn't handle one more question or one more person needing something from her.

Anita would feel so physically and mentally drained, that if one of her kids asked her a question while she was making dinner, she couldn't handle it. She explained, "I felt that I just didn't have enough to give. I'd go blank sometimes, not even knowing how to respond. Other times, I'd yell at them . . . I just wanted them to shut up . . . to stop needing me." She felt that she didn't have enough to nurture herself, much less three children.

But over the years certain things clicked for her. She began to take things less personally at work, and later changed jobs to a more professional work environment. She stopped being afraid of her ex-husband and saw him for what he was . . . irresponsible, but concerned about the kids, even if he didn't share much in their upbringing. Most remarkably, Anita learned to be in the moment, and to enjoy her life. Through an incredible amount of hard work and faith that it would eventually pay off, she became very grounded, and joyful.

This hard work included:

- Noticing her feelings or anxiety without feeling like she had to do something about it.
- Making time to be quiet: gardening, walking and meditating became a refuge for her. She also taught her children how to spend time quietly together and alone.
- Family meetings helped organize some of the chaos. There was a time and place to bring up problems, brainstorm solutions, complain, brag and work out their differences. This was a helpful tool for the whole family.

After several years of psychotherapy, Anita still reacted to extreme stress, or a lot of moderate stress happening all at once. But she was calm and grounded most of the time. She described this as, "I feel more myself. This is who I am—I feel grounded, I value my well-being and my kids' well-being more than I value having a new car, a bunch of gadgets I use for a week and put away or trying to impress my family or coworkers. I'm more clear about what I care about, and that's a less stressful way to live. I used to feel like I was supposed to care about all those other things. It's as if the real me was hiding under the stress and the impatience and feeling overwhelmed. Now I'm out and I'm not going to be buried under that crap again."

Moms at Play

A sign that you're grounded and in the present moment is if you can be playful with your children. I don't mean sitting down for a game of Scrabble. I mean the kind of playfulness that you feel when you're relaxed, and fully present, and responding in the moment without an agenda. Life stops being deadly serious when you're playful. And your kids will feel you're truly available.

E-mail from Julie

Subj: Tips for Single Moms
From: julie@bigcompany.com

- Guilt is usually a waste of time, energy and tears. Try to live in the moment. This was revolutionary for me as a separated then divorced mom. Otherwise, I was living in a state of anticipatory fear.
- Try to be smart about money. See a financial advisor for objective guidance on retirement, college savings, etc. But don't deny yourself some small things that will bring you some pleasure.
- It's OK to hold your children responsible for their behavior. Don't be surprised if they regress a bit during the separation and other aspects of the transition. But don't indulge them more than if you were with a partner.
- Try to protect your children from the tensions in your life, although having them see you as human is also OK.
- Support may come from places that surprise you, and be absent in places that hurt. Take advantage of it wherever it comes from, and work on the hurt caused by other relationships that fail you much later, when you can better handle it.

Resources for Single Mothers

- If you have parents who are loving and you can move yourself and your kids into their home, or move them out to you, this often prevents most of the typical difficulties that children in divorced families suffer. They'll have Grandpa around as a live-in male role model, and Grandma to provide lots of love when you're at work or need a break.

- Utilize community-based programs in your area that reflect your values and fill in the gaps where your child has needs. For example, Big Brother/Big Sister programs (secular and religious organizations are available in many areas) scouting programs, and other supportive services. In the Los Angeles area, there are programs that match senior citizens with children who don't have much contact with their grandparents, opportunities for children to be visited by therapy dogs, and other supportive services. Check into the resources in your community.

- Religious organizations often have resources for single-parent families. Check them out carefully, as you would any other community program. An advantage of religious programs, if you belong to that faith, is that they will reinforce your spiritual values in addition to the benefits they provide for the specific services themselves.

- Close friends can be role models for your kids and you can swap baby-sitting with those adults that you really trust. I've been "borrowing" my friend Catherine's twin girls every week for eight years now, since they were three years old. I've done volunteer projects with them, participated in their classrooms almost every year and help them with their homework after school. I can always count on them to go out for an ice cream cone when a craving hits. It's a blessing that they're part of our family, and we're part of theirs. Please consider being part of a family in your neighborhood.

Homeschooling Moms

I had such an intense emotional investment in how my daughter was doing. On a bad day it was hard to say, 'Oh well . . .' the way I think a teacher would be able to do. Plus there's no pay or vacation time. It was hard to know when we weren't 'schooling.' Every opportunity became a lesson, which can interfere with just being Mom. And all the responsibility was on me, which really played into pressuring myself and feeling inadequate at times. I'm sure most new teachers feel that pressure to 'do it right,' but when it's your own child and there's no mentor to guide you, the pressure can be overwhelming.

—BEATRICE, SAN DIEGO, CALIFORNIA

Homeschooling moms are great candidates for burnout because they've added a full-time job to their already heavy burden of responsibilities. Some of the reasons it's likely for a homeschooling mom to get burned out include the following:

• Since homeschooling is still relatively rare, moms who home-school have to field difficult questions and misguided comments from friends and family.

- Homeschooling moms don't get the break during the day that other moms get when their children are in school. They can feel overwhelmed because of their additional responsibilities that other moms share with various teachers, principal, other school staff, sports coaches, etc.
- It's easy to get burned out if their child has learning difficulties, or a different learning style than the mother.

Beatrice is a forty-year-old homeschooling mom, and a part-time marriage and family therapist. She's been homeschooling her seven-year-old daughter, Annie, for one year now, and has gotten burned out. She's going to have to make some changes in how she approaches teaching Annie or else it will feel more like a burden than the enlightening process she anticipated.

Beatrice was motivated to try homeschooling Annie for a few reasons. She had friends who loved doing it and their children were doing great now that they were out of the traditional classroom environment. Beatrice wasn't anxious to have Annie influenced by the Britney Spears wanna-be's and other negative social influences at the local public schools. And she didn't think that the local schools would be a good fit for Annie.

But things didn't go exactly as planned, and Beatrice started getting burned out after the initial excitement wore off. She explains, "The actual experience of homeschooling was not what I imagined. Most days were wonderful, but there were days when I wasn't sure if I was doing enough for Annie. I really expected her to excel in all areas as I'd seen my friends' kids do, but there were some challenging areas for her that threw me."

Still, there were more positive experiences, even lifelong memories formed, than negative ones. "I loved sharing that learning experience with Annie. It was a very special thing to share and I felt like it bonded us on another level. It's wonderful to watch your child bloom. And homeschooling made sharing her day in school much more natural. She didn't have to recount her school experience to me the way kids do when asked, 'what did you do in school today?'"

Everyone's a Critic

Mariaemma Willis, coauthor of *Discover Your Child's Learning Style: Children Learn in Unique Ways—Here's the Key to Every Child's Learning Success*, works with a lot of burned out homeschooling moms. She finds that homeschooling parents get burned out because of the stress that comes from comparing themselves to others, and hearing critical comments from friends and family. "The worst is when there's a teacher in the family," says Mariaemma. "Teachers are usually pretty shocked that parents don't have to use specific textbooks, and can choose curriculum based on their child's interests and needs. Or you have the panicky mother-in-law who's sure that you're ruining Johnny's chances of getting into college and making something of himself because you're homeschooling. Parents who don't have a teaching background, but can see that their child wasn't learning well at school, can get intimidated by these comments and pointed questions.

"I teach parents to turn these critical comments into a positive . . . 'Isn't that great that we don't need to use textbooks?! We're so free to explore all aspects of a topic.' When moms hear themselves making excuses, they're getting defensive, and they need to show their confidence, share the positive aspects of what they're doing, and then move on."

Another case of burnout that Mariaemma sees frequently is the homeschooling mom who doesn't feel qualified. At first, it can be overwhelming to put together a curriculum and balance your child's enjoyment of learning with making sure that they are being exposed to the best sources and stimulating information. "That's where the learning styles information comes in," says Mariaemma. "The more you know about how your child learns, the more competent you'll be. The bottom line is that homeschooling parents become the best teacher their child can have. I call homeschooling parents 'coaches' because you are the person who helps that child draw out and discover and develop all their interests and talents and their best potential. A teacher conveys information . . . educate really means draw out, but what we really do in classrooms is to stuff in. It's not a drawing out from the inside."

The learning styles information that Mariaemma and coauthor Victoria Hodson teach parents eliminates the constant battle many homeschooling (and other) parents have when trying to help their child learn. This is because they're working with the natural way their child learns.

Many homeschooling parents try the traditional approach even though their child already struggled in school and they know that model doesn't work. But they don't know another model. "That's when the kid will squirm and say 'I hate this!' . . . they may even tell the mother, 'I hate you!' and crumple up their paper and throw it on the floor. It feels like a constant battle. When you find out their style, the whole world opens up and it's a completely different picture," explains Mariaemma.

Detoxing

Of course, there's some lag time as you begin to understand how to help your child learn, and before they notice that your new method is different. Mariaemma says, "Not every child goes through detoxing. But some kids feel so bad about themselves from their school experience that they have a period we call 'detox.' The parent has to completely back off, or maybe just focus on a genuine interest of the child . . . if they love airplanes, take them to the airplane museum. They can integrate some educational television. Basically, they need to get them to relax and help them discover what holds their interest.

"It may take days or weeks, but then you've got a whole different kid who is now developing some curiosity and seeing learning as fun . . . eventually this will turn into a love of learning for it's own sake."

Too Much of a Good Thing

Mariaemma sees a lot of moms like Beatrice, who are burned out in part because they are the one person responsible for their child's education. "One of the first things we tell parents is that you don't have to do this by yourself," Mariaemma explains. "It's better if you're part of a team. Identify other people who will be on your team."

Mariaemma recommends:

- Divide up the work, like a co-op, with other parents who homeschool. Swap days, or parts of a day, for example.
- Use the talents of other parents. If one parent sews, that parent teaches sewing. If another parent is a scientist, they bring their expertise to that subject.
- Find classes in the community, for example in Ventura County

a company called "Mad Science" does a fun but educational science program through the parks and recreation department. There are ballet, music, karate and theater classes in most communities. A lot of these programs offer classes during the day because there are more homeschoolers than ever.

• Get your child involved in outside activities, organized sports, 4-H, scouts, etc.

• Even if your husband doesn't have time to be a primary teacher he can help with homework or special projects so the child gets input from both parents.

Mariaemma continues, "When any parent is discouraged about their child, they focus on what is wrong with them. They often tell me a long list of things their child is struggling with: he's disorganized, he doesn't like to read, he doesn't like math, etc. I have the parent make a list of everything that is wonderful about their child . . . any talent they have, any interest. It's so amazing. Parents will call or e-mail me and say, 'Thank you so much, I have a completely different view of my child! I can't believe I couldn't see all the great things about him, and that I was so focused on the negatives.' Then they can start over."

Mariaemma's
"What's Good About My Child"
Journaling Exercise

Make a list of all the things your child is good at, things that have nothing to do with school or academic learning. Include natural talents and skills, personality characteristics and things your child is passionate about.

_____

_____

_____

_____

_____

_____

_____

_____

_____

_____

_____

_____

_____

_____

_____

_____

_____

_____

Parenting a Special-Needs Child

Parenting any child is an experience that makes us grow, which means it pushes us beyond our comfort zone. Parenting a special-needs child can push us too far, and instead of feeling that we're rising to the occasion of meeting our child's needs, we instead feel overwhelmed, disappointed and frustrated.

"The parents of special-needs children have a deeper road because their losses are more traumatic," explains Joan Maltese, Ph.D., a clinical psychologist and cofounder and executive director of the Child Development Institute in Woodland Hills, California. "They have more than just the frustrations of parenting and understanding their child. They have to deal with a child that often can't be taught to read without a team of experts."

Stages Parents Go Through

"These parents at first feel hopeless and frustrated as they see that their child isn't meeting the developmental milestones, or their communication is not coming in, or they have challenges where other children don't. The pain of seeing your child suffering with these burdens is terrible."

A typical family, according to Dr. Maltese, is one in which the father isn't convinced that there is something wrong with his child, and the mother is burned out because she's coordinating doctor appointments, locating resources, and handling most or all of the day-to-day child care with a child who is hard to tune into and gets frustrated easily. And she doesn't have the support of her husband if he's in denial, and possibly doesn't have anyone else she can talk to about her worries and difficulties.

Dr. Maltese's program for families of special-needs children provides parent support groups for parents with newly diagnosed children. She points out, "The other parents are so helpful to the
newcomers. They remember when they first joined the group and
were just devastated and felt alone, and they have so much
strength and hope to share with new group members."

After you've gone through the denial, shock, and disappointment and grief process of realizing that your child has special needs
and that your mother's intuition isn't always enough to understand
how to respond to your child, there's an opening. Dr. Maltese
describes this as the time when the parents shift their focus from
what their child *can't* do to what
she *can* do. "The process of griev-
ing deeply for the loss of who you
hoped your child would be is very
important. It takes a long time.
When parents come to a full
acceptance of what is, and who
their child is, they appreciate

[Parents of special-needs
children] feel incredible joy . . .
they have waited years for their
child to say, "Mommy" or
"Daddy."

everything their child can do and experience. They feel incredible
joy . . . they have waited years for their child to say, 'Mommy' or
'Daddy.' They really celebrate these incremental steps."

Dr. Maltese finds that once parents get involved with their
child's treatment, they often become the best advocates for their
children and others' children with special needs. "One father of
a two-year-old with autism spectrum disorder (which includes
delayed speech, stereotypical behavior and a lack of social-
emotional connection) didn't want anyone to know about his
child's challenges at first. He talked about 'those children' and
distanced himself from his son. Now, a year after the initial

diagnosis, he makes it a point to raise others' sensitivity and compassion for special-needs children and their families."

What should you do if your child's development seems slower than her peers, or if she has a hard time soothing herself or handling even low levels of stress?

1. See your child's pediatrician for an exam and a referral to a specialist if necessary.
2. Early intervention can help your child avoid future problems, and can help you get the information and support you need to alleviate parenting burnout or prevent it.

Dr. Maltese's Tips for Parents Caring for a Special-Needs Child:

1. **Help your child regulate his feelings.**

   When your child is upset, first pay attention to why he is overwhelmed. Was he seeking or avoiding sensory input of some kind? For example, if your child is throwing himself on the floor, he may want sensory stimulation. Once you've determined this is what he needs, give him that stimulation to help him get regulated—for example, gently but firmly press on his hands or feet. This will calm him down. Once he's calmer, he can do what he was attempting to do when he got upset—transition to another activity, or meet a guest in your home, for example.

2. **Get support from other families and friends.**

   You can only do this if you're honest with them about your child. Get involved in a parent support group, educate your spouse and extended family so that they'll better understand your child's needs as well as what you're going through. Some programs offer help educating the support system of primary caregivers.

Having a positive support system is critical in coping with parenting burnout.

3. **Have your own life.**

It's common for mothers to put their children's needs first and neglect their own life. But with a special-needs child, moms typically have an even harder time setting boundaries, taking time for herself and being a wife, not just a mom. If you're a whole person and have a strong and loving marriage, you give your child the security and stability he needs.

4. **Let your child express his needs before you jump in to meet them.**

Your child will feel respected, will become better at communicating his needs and he'll increase his ability to tolerate frustration.

PART THREE

CREATING YOUR SYNERGY PLAN

CHAPTER SIX

Synergy Planning Begins with Getting Focused

*"I had never planned what I'd have
for dinner, much less a business plan that
would have a long-term vision. My only business
plan to date had been to make money to pay
the bills by training dogs. When I was through,
I had a great plan to keep me focused for
years to come. I recently revised my plan
to include some new aspects to my dog-training
business: rescuing dogs from the pound and
training them to be bomb detection dogs,
doing seminars and selling equipment."*

—ELAINE ALLISON, OWNER OF
CANINE'S BEST BEHAVIOR, LOS ANGELES

I've probably written more articles on getting and staying focused than on any other single topic. I think this is partly because it's so important to living a purposeful life. If you allow

145

your mind to be scattered and stay on the surface, you won't discover your unique path. I think it's also because it's so hard to do. Especially for creative people. We have way too many ideas to focus on just one. We start out with good intentions. We psych ourselves up to stay with one idea and follow through on it. But almost immediately we think of something else we'd like to do, and say to ourselves, "I can't pursue that now . . . I've got to stay focused." Then we remember another idea we've always wanted to try and think . . . "Now I have to miss out on that, too."

Pretty soon, the goal of getting and staying focused that seemed the solution to our frustrating history of scattered ideas and wasted energy is causing us to feel deprived and as if someone put blinders on us. Fortunately, just like in relationships, eventually deepening our commitment to one path is ultimately much more rewarding than continually keeping our options open and staying on the surface.

Some of the reasons we lose our focus:

- We have lots of interests
- We don't like to say no to projects or requests for favors
- We're easily distracted
- We're so busy, we stay on the surface of life just trying to get through the day
- If we do try to focus, we too often choose a superficial project that's not connected to our true self. This leads to boredom, being easily distracted, and burnout.

In this chapter, I'll offer some tips for getting and staying focused. Then I'll discuss why planning is not only important but can be enjoyable. Finally, I'll share several Synergy Planning worksheets to help you get started on your path.

"Synergy" means an outcome that is greater than the sum of its parts. Your Synergy Plan will get you on track for personal and business success as you define it. It's your road map for becoming "inwardly mobile." Another reason I use the term "synergy" for this action plan is because it lets you find and resolve incompatible goals and values that almost all of us have as we plan our career paths. For example, you may start your own business in order to have more control over your schedule, but your marketing produces such fast growth that you barely have time to eat and sleep.

There Are Many Paths, but You Can Only Follow One at a Time

Dr. Moody, in his book about the stages of soul development that I mentioned in chapter 1, tells of an experience that led him out of being overwhelmed by all of the possible paths he could follow, and showed him the wisdom of making a commitment to one choice.

> Years ago I wandered into a New Age bookshop in the Upper West Side of Manhattan and ended up having a lively conversation with the manager. A man approximately my age, he had converted to Islam a decade earlier and entered a Sufi order. Seeing the motley collection of spiritual books I was toting, he looked at me with a bemused smile. "I see you've been caught by the candy store," he remarked.
>
> "What do you mean?" I asked.
>
> "All the goodies on one big shelf," he said, looking at my selection. "The Kabbalah, Esoteric Christianity, Gurdjieff, est, Theosophy. It's hard not to want them all at once, isn't it?"

I had to agree.

"But you know," he added, "for me and the other members of our group our search is over. We've found what we're looking for. We don't need to read all these books anymore or make the rounds at the meetings. Our way gives us everything we need."

I didn't particularly like what this man was saying. I felt I'd heard it before: the sense of unquestioned conviction, the cool-headed surety. Yet there was also a disturbing ring of truth to what he said: "Our way gives us everything we need." These words aroused mixed emotions in me, and not a little envy as I stood there embarrassed, holding half a dozen books under my arm. For a moment I felt a little like an unmarried guest in a room full of happily married people. Why can't I find a commitment that satisfies me fully? I wondered. Like this man.

Almost immediately the answer flashed through my mind: because something in me doesn't really want to commit, doesn't really want to take the responsibility for my own spiritual destiny. I was, if the truth be known, having too good a time browsing the spiritual candy store. . . . And so my search went on.[23]

I find it ironic that for many of us it feels natural to choose not just one *career*, but one *job*, but when it comes to pursuing our calling, variety feels safer than commitment. There are so many books, meetings, groups and even organized religions vying for our attention. In West Hollywood near Los Angeles there is a New

---

[23] Moody, Harry R., Ph.D., and David Carroll. *The Five Stages of the Soul: Charting the Spiritual Passages That Shape Our Lives.* New York: Anchor/Doubleday, 1997. pp. 159–160.

Age bookstore called The Boddhi Tree, named after the tree under which the Buddha sat when he became enlightened. There are books, tapes, jewelry and accessories of all kinds representing every faith, path and practice known to man. And near the UFO section and not too far from the books on a variety of conspiracy theories, there's even a shelf labeled, "Speculation."

The Boddhi Tree is the West Coast version of the spiritual candy store. I'm very curious about a lot of ideas and religions, and while there's value in learning about different philosophies and religions, I can forget that this is just intellectual knowledge if I stay on the surface as an observer not a participant. I can learn about other faiths, but I can't become a devotee of more than one at a time. The word "devotee" itself implies that I *devote* myself to one path. If my goal is to live by a spiritual teaching, not just to collect some clever anecdotes to use in my lectures, I have to start down one path and go where it leads me.

How to Enjoy Getting Focused

There are several ways to make getting and staying focused easier.

- Turn *toward something positive*, as opposed to only *turning away from the negative*. The usual distractions and other elements that drain your energy will still be there, but you'll have a reason to stay focused. This makes it easier to ignore the distractions.
- Try to get some insight into *why* you struggle to focus. When you know what gets in your way, you can take a step back and look at these issues in a more detached and objective way.

Instead of getting swept up in a flood of activities, you can keep a healthy perspective on what's pulling you away from being grounded and on track.

- Pay attention to how you spend your time and stop allowing yourself to waste time on unworthy projects. If your teenage daughter had a big test tomorrow, and you saw her doing everything *but* prepare for the test, you'd probably point out that she's wasting the time she needs to use to study. How can you make sure that you first take care of what you most need to do? What advice would you give your daughter or best friend?

Contrary to popular belief, downtime is not wasted time. But spending your most valuable resource (time) on something that isn't extremely important to you *is* a waste of time.

- Stand for something. Getting focused has a lot to do with your mission. Your mission should be the foundation of your various intentions and activities. If you spend your time, attention and other resources on what furthers your mission, you'll feel good about how you're spending your time.
- Create conditions in your life to allow you to focus on what you most care about:
  - Eliminate unnecessary activities.
  - Reduce your overhead.
  - Learn to enjoy downtime without feeling "unproductive."
  - Don't do projects simply because you feel obligated.
  - Don't say "yes" to anything right away.
  - Share your mission with others so they can alert you to opportunities.

How Do I Make a Living While I'm Pursuing What I Love to Do?

How do you do something you love *and* make a living? One way to meet this challenge is to include your different interests and needs as you write your career goals and guidelines.

Maybe your job is a reflection of the serious, sensible you. Sometimes we're too "businesslike" when we plan our career, forgetting that there are other aspects of our personality that we can draw on to make a more balanced plan. Are there other aspects of your personality that you can express within your current career path?

Most of us still have to pay bills while pursuing our calling. A wonderful book called *Creating a Life Worth Living* addresses this in detail. Author Carol Lloyd interviewed dozens of creative people and asked them how they earned enough to cover their overhead when they were in the early stages of trying to make a living from their creative work. She also offers advice to help readers discover which creative career will truly satisfy them. "Once you accept the fact that you have needs outside your art, you can begin to craft a life that will survive the hardships of a creative career."[24] I'd add that you have to accept the fact that you have needs outside your *work*.

Trail Marker: *Identify as many of your needs as you can, both work- and non-work-related. Consider all of them as you plan your path.*

---

[24] Lloyd, Carol. *Creating a Life Worth Living: A Practical Course in Career Design for Artists, Innovators, and Others Aspiring to a Creative Life*. New York: HarperPerennial, 1997. p. 94.

You can follow your calling and create a marketable business with some planning and research. The prerequisite is to first feel connected to your mission, then to notice what you are drawn toward. Once you have this solid foundation you can do the market research to find out how to express your calling and deep interests in the concrete form of a career path. (Doing market research basically involves determining who your market is and learning as much as you can about their needs, expectations and ability to afford your product or service. You'll also research what the competition is doing; fee ranges and profit margins in your field; and how to best reach your target market.)

Do you have some ideas for a business, but don't yet have the resources to get started? Or are you intrigued by the thought of having your own business, but you're not exactly sure what kind of business or how to get started? Carol Lloyd's book, as well as others listed in the resource list at the end of this book, can help.

There are several steps to making a living at what you love to do, all of them necessary:

1. Listen to your calling and create your Mission Statement (see page 161.)
2. Discover ways to translate your calling into marketable skills.
3. Learn which starving markets relate to your calling and skills.
4. Create a strategy to approach and enter that starving market.
5. Fine-tune your plan: Make necessary adjustments as you get feedback from the market and from your reactions to what you're doing that you most enjoy, and don't enjoy.

It's Risky Business Without a Plan

When I started my first consulting business, I asked my brother-in-law, Jack, what to do. I had a "great idea" and I was anxious to get started. Should I first find rental space for the parenting resource center I envisioned? Or should I hire some staff first? Jack told me to write a business plan.

I'd never even thought about writing a business plan before, and I had no idea how to write one. So I did what I always do when I need to learn a new skill . . . I went to the library and came home with a five-feet tall pile of books. I think I went through that stack of business planning books in two weeks, I was so excited about the whole process. Then I started doing my market research, checked costs on all the big and small items and wrote up a sample schedule for the facility I hoped would give new parents a supportive and fun environment for them and their children. It would be a place where they could learn the latest information about bonding and attachment, where they could meet other parents and talk about the challenges of raising children and where they could get some answers to their parenting questions so they wouldn't feel overwhelmed and resort to doing whatever might give them some relief in the short term but cause problems later on.

About three months later I had written my plan and crunched the numbers. But something was very, very wrong. No matter what I adjusted, I couldn't figure out a way to make a profit. And on top of that, my research told me that a lot of local medical groups were offering some of the services I would have to charge for, like parenting classes, for free.

I was really disappointed. I had my heart set on the Parenting Center, as I was calling it in my plan. About a month after I gave up on the idea, I heard about the very same business as I had planned starting up blocks away from the property I had checked out for my Parenting Center. I was really surprised. I wanted to know how they figured out a way to make it work. They offered just what I had planned—parenting classes, story time and workshops given by experts on topics of interest to parents. So how did they figure out a way to make a profit?

Eighteen months later I got my answer. They'd closed due to lack of funds. I realized that they must not have written a business plan, at least not one with real numbers. I felt really awful for the owners, imagining how much of their heart and soul went into their failed project. They must have been incredibly disappointed, and I assume they took a financial loss.

I think of that experience whenever I talk to a client who doesn't want to write a thorough, accurate business plan. I've found that most of my clients who balk at writing a plan start to enjoy the research and planning once I give them specific tasks to do. And if they don't find the process interesting or enjoyable, they'll find out that their business idea doesn't sustain their enthusiasm *before* they invest their time, money and hard work in a business that isn't a good match for them.

Elaine Allison, the dog trainer quoted at the beginning of this chapter, reacted like a lot of my clients. She didn't think about writing a business plan until she needed a loan. In her case it was to buy property to grow her dog-training business. "At first, it was completely overwhelming, and it seemed like all the books and Web sites on business planning were in another language. With help, it actually became a fun thing. I could let my imagination fly! And because I had to write my plan, I came up with things I hadn't even considered before."

Bring Your Future into the Present: Balancing Short- and Long-Term Goals

Do you feel that you should pursue your calling, but you have bills to pay, family responsibilities and other day-to-day concerns that don't allow you to stop everything to do so . . . even if you knew what you're called to do?

How do you take care of your immediate needs without letting go of a meaningful future? And how can working little by little toward your future make your *daily* life more meaningful?

> ❀
>
> The more you feel pulled toward your calling, the less you'll have to push, and pushing is much harder work.

Creating *both* a short-term plan for day-to-day needs *and* a long-term plan to accomplish what you really care about is the answer. The secret is to break your long-term plan into small pieces that you can integrate into your daily schedule.

The Short Term

Having a short-term plan is critical when you have bills to pay because it allows you to be productive while you're planning for a more meaningful future. If you're searching for your calling, a short-term plan will include a "day job" that pays the bills so you don't have to figure out what you should be doing with your life by the end of the month so you can afford to pay the mortgage.

Integrate the Long Term

Working toward your long-term plan every day gives meaning to those daily activities. It's also important to build momentum toward that long-term plan so you feel pulled toward it as it becomes more real every day. The more you feel pulled toward your calling, the less you'll have to push, and pushing is much harder work.

Tips for Short- and Long-Term Planning

Here are some tips that might be useful as you clarify your long-range goals and plans, and take care of current responsibilities.

1. **Make long-term planning a *priority*.**

   It's very hard to stay focused on "important but not-urgent" aspects of our life, to use Steven Covey's term. All planning based on our values falls into this category. We're usually busy with "urgent, not important" items, like ringing phones, e-mail and requests from others. It's easy to postpone planning the most important aspects of our lives until we are no longer living our lives "on purpose."

2. **Fit long-term planning into your *daily life*.**

   Set aside a little time on a regular basis. Don't wait until you have lots of time. Squeeze it in whenever you have a half an hour. You'll create momentum, and get more done this way.

   A client of mine, Terry, is making a dramatic career change from doing Web site design to being a massage therapist. She needs to inquire about training programs and create a network to find out what it's really like to do this kind of work, what schools have the best programs and how to eventually get referrals and start a practice.

   She's managed to carve out half an hour during her work day to pursue her new career. So each day she sends off a couple of e-mails, makes a phone call or two or does some reading.

"I was concerned at first that using my lunch hour to do my coaching homework would make me *more* stressed out," Terry told me recently. "But I feel more enthusiastic now that I see I'm getting somewhere. Every day I'm doing something that gets me closer to my dream of being a massage therapist, and I really think I'm going to be able to do it."

3. **Remind yourself often *why* you care about your long-term plans.**

The hardest time in any career transition is the first few months. If you're like many people I talk to in transition:

- You have an idea that you've avoided acting on for a long time.
- You don't have a track record (or it's limited) for doing what you dream about doing.
- You may doubt whether what you dream about will ever become a reality.

In other words, you have a vague idea of a road ahead, and lots of roadblocks. That makes for a bumpy ride.

By reminding yourself why you care about your dream you'll strengthen your connection to it, and refresh your motivation to get there.

Once you start taking the first small steps on your career path, you'll discover more and more reasons why your path is right for you. Most important you'll discover that the best opportunities for you come once you're on your path. These are the ones that you couldn't have anticipated ahead of time but appear once you have made the commitment to your path. (I'll discuss this in more depth in chapter 8.)

It's easy to get lost in the daily details of life. It's also easy to keep our dreams safely in the future, not spoiling their "perfection" by acting on them.

The key to living based on your calling in each moment is to bring your future plans into the present little by little. Doing bits and pieces of your long-term plans, with the overall map in mind, will bring you closer to your calling being part of your daily life.

Your Mission Statement Gives You Roots in What Is Meaningful to You

Most planning processes use only our practical side. That side of us:

- Is concerned with getting things done
- Uses tools like agendas and to-do lists
- Is based on the left side of the brain (the logical, language-based side)

As we've been discussing, our true self or soul is that part of us that is connected to our intuition (which is based in our right brain, the side which uses images and is more holistic) and is able to tune into whatever wisdom we're capable of. Our soul is concerned with:

- What is true and real, beneath appearances
- A deeper connection with others
- Eternal questions, like "What is the meaning of our lives?" and "How can we best fulfill our purpose?"

If we ignore our spiritual side, we can come up with a practical plan, but we'll eventually feel as if we're missing something important no matter how outwardly successful we become. And if we ignore our practical side, we might be able to identify what we're passionate about, but we won't be able to bring it to fruition.

Sometimes people who think mostly with their right brain, like artists or musicians, complement their talents by partnering with a businessperson to direct the practical side of their life. This kind of partnership can be successful, but if you'd like to get *both* halves of your brain working together, you have to call upon each side to do what it does best. The right side, which uses intuitive, holistic thinking, will be the best side to call upon to stay grounded in who you really are and to make sure you will continue to find your path meaningful and satisfying. And you should use your left brain or logical side when it's time to spell out the steps and write a concrete plan that you can transfer into your calendar.

Most of us have more natural ability on either the left or the right brain side. So we favor that side. But just because it feels more comfortable to write a to-do list than to do the necessary soul-searching, that doesn't mean that's what we ought to do. (Even your left brain would agree with that logic!)

Draft Your Mission Statement

Use the worksheet on page 161 to begin to create your Mission Statement. If you already have one, take this opportunity to review it and revise it as necessary.

When you first create your Mission Statement, you should plan on reviewing it every couple of weeks for a few months. After that, review it every six months to make sure it still reflects your mission so it will help you stay focused. You can use your Mission Statement when various opportunities come your way as a guide to rule out those that will get you off track even though they sound enticing on the surface.

Even though I'm asking you to start the Synergy Planning process with your Mission Statement, you'll find that after you fill out your Family & Personal Goals and Guideposts and your Career & Business Goals and Guideposts worksheets is a good time to revise your Mission Statement. These worksheets are most effective when you use the Mission Statement to get you grounded on a general principle, then use the two Goals and Guideposts worksheets to get very specific about how to express that mission. That's why after you work on the specifics, it makes sense to go back to your mission and make sure these specifics are contained in your statement. The various worksheets spell out both the macro and the micro aspirations of your career and life, so there's always a dynamic tension between them.

Synergy Plan℠ Worksheet:
Mission Statement

1. Chapter 1 discussed listening to your calling. What do you think might be your calling? Note any hunches, ideas and intuitions. Don't worry about whether or not you can connect your calling with a paying position at this point. Your calling is probably not a job title.

_____

_____

_____

_____

2. Who's affected by your mission? What problem will you solve for them?

For example: I want to help people in midlife who are burned out to take advantage of this condition as a wake-up call and discover a healthier relationship with work and themselves that makes them a deeper person, provides them with a more meaningful life and prevents them from becoming burned out again.

_____

_____

_____

_____

3. Action words that describe your mission?

For example: facilitate, coach, brighten, communicate, educate, explore, discover, inspire, write.

_____

_____

_____

_____

4. Write a first draft of your Mission Statement, stringing together the action words and the specifics about what you'd like to do to be of service or what problem you'd like to solve with your business or career. Start with phrases. Then write sentences that your mother, high school teacher, or your neighbor would understand and would make them feel that you have a cause you believe in.

_____

_____

_____

_____

Sample Mission Statements

Elaine Allison, Dog Trainer: We are compassionate, caring trainers who help owner and dog have a greater relationship through humane, benevolent leadership and structure, ultimately preventing backyard banishment, re-homing or eventual euthanasia with concise solution-based information. I will also use my temperament assessment and dog training abilities to train suitable dogs that have been banished to the pound to do bomb detection work.

Shirley Oya, Money Coach: To help families learn to manage their finances so they can keep more of what they earn and spend more time doing what they value most in life.

Mary Mora, Trainer: As the training coordinator for Jan S.T.A.R., a staff training company, I base my sales and marketing campaigns on the belief that by offering our programs to clients at any level in their company, anyone can achieve their career goals and enhance their quality of life with the proper training provided by a professionals who teach their clients to perform at their peak level.

Other examples:

Tutor: To teach kids (and their parents) that learning is fun, and prepare them for a lifetime of loving to learn.

Freelance Business Writer: To use my writing abilities to highlight businesses that treat employees well and use integrity in their interactions with clients.

My Mission Statement: To help people become inwardly mobile and base their work and lives on their true self or soul, and to live my own life on that basis.

Family & Personal Goals and Guideposts

Now that you've begun to draft the foundation for all of your planning, your Mission Statement, let's turn to your family and personal goals and guideposts. I use the term "guideposts" here because there are two functions for these worksheets. One is to identify your goals—what you aspire to do, change or accomplish. The other is to make sure you stay on track once you're starting on your path. A guidepost can be as general as putting your young children before your career until they're older. Or you can spell out the ones that you want to be especially conscious of, for example: to be home most evenings and weekends, to transition your children from day care to staying home with you in a certain amount of time or to pick up your children from school most days. But the point is that these aren't just goals. They're guideposts that can tell you if you're veering off course, or if you're on the right track, if you notice them as you go by.

I ask clients to spell out their family and personal goals and guideposts before their career or business goals, since women who are burned out (or at risk of burnout) have neglected themselves, and many haven't put their family first when it comes to their behavior.

If you have children, you already know that you have to put their needs before your own in many ways. But if you always put yourself last, you won't have much to give them. If you're often impatient, overtired and distracted, you can't give them what they need emotionally.

Children of all ages need parents who understand and respond to their needs. (I list books for parents of young children in the resource section for chapter 5 at the end of the book.) But preteens and teenagers need a loving adult to be there when they get home from school and to help them struggle to do the right and moral thing when their peers pressure them to do otherwise. It's important to know your children's friends and their families, and to supervise their social life.

I realize that I may come across as being from some ideal planet where moms can do all these things. But I'm describing what your child needs. We can't always meet each of our children's needs, but if we know what they are, we can make meeting those needs a priority and do the best we can.

I've helped a lot of mothers write both a short-term plan and a long-term plan when they can't be as available as their children need them to be right away (as I described on pages 155–158.) But if we only focus on *what we can do right now*, we'll ignore the reality of our children's needs, as well as our own.

I've included my Family & Personal Goals and Guideposts Worksheet on page 167 for you to fill out. You may want to consider how your husband, extended family, close friends, and other available resources can help you bridge the gap between what you're currently *able* to do and what you and your family's needs *actually* are.

Don't Neglect Your Marriage

I've been neglecting your husband so far in this section because I've been so intent on pointing out your children's needs. But I believe that if you're married, your husband should actually be your top priority. Your marriage is the foundation of your family. Your family members are like building blocks. If you and your husband are each emotionally healthy, secure and loving, you'll have a strong marriage. If you have a strong, loving marriage, you'll be able to offer an invaluable sense of stability to your children, extended family and your community.

There are sound reasons that our husbands' needs often get put on the back burner, especially if we have children. Most husbands have more frustration tolerance than an infant. Add to that a new mom's hormonally charged instinct to form a bond with her baby, and you're on your way to a family structure that's upside down. We women have to work very hard to be wives and women, and not just mommies. Our husbands can help remind us that we're women and wives if we let them.

Synergy Plan℠ Worksheet: Family & Personal Goals and Guideposts

Write your two or three family and personal guideposts (the total of all goals on this page should not be more than three).

For example: spend days with children until 4 P.M. when husband gets home; spend 1:1 time with six-year-old every Saturday morning; work from home 9 A.M. to noon 5 days a week; eat dinner together 4 times a week; have family meetings every Tuesday; walk dog every day before work for 40 minutes; set aside an hour twice a week to paint.

1. _____
   _____
   _____
   _____
   _____

2. _____
   _____
   _____
   _____
   _____

3. _____
   _____
   _____
   _____
   _____

What will the short-term look like? What does a typical day, evening and weekend look like? Do you have breakfast, lunch or dinner together? Do you have family meetings? How much time do you spend together on family activities, and how much time do you all get to spend on individual activities and relaxing? How much do you travel for pleasure? Write whatever describes the picture accurately to you as you visualize your life as you'd like it to be in the next six months.

_____

_____

_____

_____

What about in five years? What will your personal and family life look like once you're well into your new plan?

_____

_____

_____

BOTTOM LINE: (This is where you sum up the most important lesson you need to learn from this worksheet so you can quickly and easily remind yourself what's the bottom line.)

For example: I need to pay more attention to my physical health and well-being, and make more time for my kids, my husband and myself.

_____

_____

_____

Career & Business Goals and Guideposts

My original Mission Statement when I was first started using these worksheets was: "To provide parents with the information and support they needed to understand their child's needs so they could make the best decisions about how to meet those needs within their values and the circumstances of their family."

I had found in my work as a marriage, family and child therapist, and from my parenting classes, that if people understand their child's needs, they'll make good decisions about how to meet those needs. That was the premise behind the Parenting Center. But I didn't know what else I could do to accomplish that mission.

Now, it's clear to me that the details don't matter that much as long as I'm on my path and using my skills and talents in a way that I enjoy and find challenging. It's certainly true in my role as a writer. I have a point of view and a message I want to share with others. But I can write more than one article or more than one book. There are many ways I can express myself. Each project is just one way to accomplish my mission.

In my work as a coach, I help my clients learn how to brainstorm several different jobs or business ideas. I'll go over the initial steps of this process right now. And later on, in chapter 8, I'll show you why I found that traditional goal-setting methods are limiting. Instead of having your *destination* as your goal, make *being on your unique path* your goal. That way, you'll turn up opportunities that you couldn't have planned for. And these are usually the best ones.

E-mail from Julie

Subj: Came up with idea to volunteer at my
      alma mater
From: julie@bigcompany.com

Hi Leslie,

Thanks for your last e-mail.

My husband, whom I have been secretly thinking an unsupportive, self-interested blackguard for
not making my career crisis his #1 priority, actually
came up with a fabulous idea!

I found my graduate business school incredibly
helpful in aiding alumni in job searches, networking,
career transitions, etc. They said all the right
things, but had practically no resources to put any
muscle behind their words. Well, Joe's thought was
to volunteer my services to aid them in putting
together a first class alumni career counseling
service, with the blessings of the university
corporation.

I gain the experience, and maybe they can then
help me better. I bounced this idea off the class
secretary, who started foaming at the mouth about
how overdue this was, and I already have several
volunteers.

Wasn't that a great idea? I am beginning to understand that what I want is not necessarily another job in my industry at all, but something that is more related to my skills and to functions rather than industry. And definitely with some flexibility so I can continue to enjoy my four-year-old son and give time to the bread baking I love to do.

So that's it! I will work on it a little more and see what comes of it.

All the best,

Julie

—·—·—·—·—·—·—·—·—·—·—·—·—·—·—·—·—·—·—

Dear Julie,

I love your insight into how you wanted your husband to make your "crisis" his priority! Not many people get past that.

Thanks for the update. Whatever project you end up doing is actually less important than how you approach it. You've switched gears and are using an approach that will serve you well no matter what you end up doing!

Don't worry about how it will all turn out. Just put one foot in front of the other, and stay close to what feels exciting, interesting and helpful. Then something good will result. It will take on a life of its own, which you can't anticipate, and can only

172 ❀ PART THREE: CREATING YOUR SYNERGY PLAN

interfere with! This may not even be what you will
end up doing, since it could lead to something else
you like better. These things just don't abide by our
narrow vision. I can't tell you how thankful I am
that I have never gotten what I wanted back when
I used to wish for certain outcomes!

Take care,
Leslie

Synergy Plan℠ Worksheet:
Career & Business Goals and Guideposts

1. What are the issues you care about or problems you want to solve? List as many as you can in five minutes. Refer to your journal if you've been keeping one. Or start keeping a journal in which you record brief notes about what captures your interest when you're reading, watching TV, browsing in a bookstore, etc.

_____

_____

_____

_____

2. What talents do you have? What comes naturally to you and is enjoyable?

For example: Are you good at coordinating colors and patterns? Are you a good listener? Are you funny? Concise?

_____

_____

_____

_____

What skills have you developed?

For example: Are you a good writer? Are you good at public speaking? Are you good at sales? Are you friendly and enjoy talking to people? Do you have teaching skills? Break down your job skills into basic elements. Teachers are good at hundreds of things. Don't just list "teaching skills" . . . note that you can handle speaking to a group of easily distracted people, you can make boring topics interesting, you are good at helping people enjoy learning, you are patient, etc.

_____

_____

_____

_____

3. Who will pay you for what you do?

For example, when I wanted to help parents understand their child's needs, I originally focused on a population of parents who would be motivated and able to pay for classes and other services at my Parenting Center. After I gave up the idea of starting my own facility, I did some research and found that medical groups and some employers were willing and motivated to pay for these resources to offer them to parents.

_____

_____

_____

_____

_____

1. What Do You Care About/ What Problem Do You Want to Solve

2. Skills/Talents

3. Who Will Pay/ Opportunities

There will be an area within the three circles where they overlap. By focusing on this area where these three important elements overlap, you'll make sure each of them are included. (Keep your Mission Statement and your Family & Personal Goals and Guideposts in mind here, too. Your mission is the foundation on which you build any career path specifics, and your Family & Personal Goals and Guideposts will keep you on track so you won't sabotage these priorities.) Think about how you can use your skills and talents, and your contacts and the current business climate and professional opportunities that you are currently aware of, and use those as vehicles for your mission or what you care about.

❀ EXERCISE: Turn your kitchen (or any) timer on for fifteen minutes. Get out your journal and write down as many specific opportunities as you can think of until the timer goes off. Write down the really horrible ones, the improbable ones, and the ridiculous ones. Just keep writing for fifteen minutes. By the time you finish the exercise, you may have two or three half-decent ideas. Write those in your journal when you're done.

Whatever you do, don't critique your ideas while you're brainstorming! You can't edit and write at the same time. Neither can you brainstorm and critique your ideas simultaneously.

Write your two or three most interesting business/career ideas from the brainstorming experiment above:

1. _____

_____

2. _____

_____

3. _____

_____

What will the start-up or initial transition look like? What does a typical workday look like? How often do you work on evenings or weekends? What type of work is done during off-hours and why? What is your family doing while you are working? Do you work from home at all? Are you in control of your schedule? How much do you travel for business? Is this enjoyable or stressful? Write whatever describes the picture accurately to you as you visualize your life as you'd like it to be in the next six months.

What do you want to include:

_____

_____

_____

What do you want to avoid:

_____

_____

What about in five years? What does it look like once it's up and running smoothly?

_____

_____

BOTTOM LINE: (This is where you sum up the most important lesson you need to learn from this worksheet so you can quickly and easily remind yourself what's the bottom line.)

For example: I want a flexible schedule and to work with people interested in changing their spending habits to create a better life for them and their family.

_____

_____

_____

E-mail from Julie

Subj: Lots happening!
From: julie@bigcompany.com

Dear Leslie:

Remember how worried I was about getting the training work? Well, that has taken on a life of its own. It reminds me of my sourdough starter after being fed too much flour. The outplacement firm is now going to add me to their list of trainers, I am exploring a possible affiliation with a Web-based human resources group here in NY, and I'm having so much fun! Lots of money yet? Well, no, but I can sense that it's all going in the right direction.

Anyway, this week I have lots of stuff going on. Yesterday I was in Connecticut presenting; tomorrow back here in NYC; last week I had two trainings in Massachusetts! Next week one in New Jersey, then three more scheduled after that!

All the best,
Julie

Playing with an Idea to Test It Out

When you choose a good enough starting point, you need to free your mind to experiment, or play with, this option. A lot of my clients get stuck at this point. I'll describe how conferences can be used as a concentrated version of learning and experimenting with your first opportunity. Conferences give you access to a large number of professionals in your chosen field, often in a resort setting. But you can use the ideas below without going to a conference. The process is basically the same. You would spread these steps out over a longer period of time to test out your starting point idea.

Conferences Are a Great Shortcut to Learning About a New Field

When you start to do research on your new field to find out about new developments and available opportunities, look for professional organizations in your intended field. These organizations will almost always meet for annual conferences. These are usually held in accessible parts of the country, often in resorts or locations conducive to family vacations. (Look for local chapters of these organizations in order to network with local professionals on a regular basis in your community.)

Annual conferences give you a quick way to learn a lot about your intended field, including:

- What the people in the field are like
- What kinds of opportunities are available
- What the work in that field looks like once you have paid your dues

- What additional training or education you'll *actually* need
- How much experienced professionals in the field get paid, how much control over their schedule they have, how many hours they have to work and other quality of life issues.

I've had clients get into certain fields after going to conferences. I've also had clients decide not to pursue a particular field because they realized that the type of work or circumstances were a poor match for their personalities or skills, or didn't support their mission.

At first, I was concerned that the clients who spent their money and time at a conference only to realize that this line of work wasn't for them would be disappointed and discouraged. Instead, the opposite was true. They were grateful that they found out in four days what might have taken them four years to realize if they'd gone back to school, or if they had started on the lowest rung of the ladder and assumed that things would get better if they just kept at it. Once you have years of time and thousands of dollars invested in a new career, it's a lot harder to be objective and change course midstream.

Get the Most Out of a Conference

Here are some tips I've given clients over the years about how to get the most return on investment at conferences.

A few weeks before the conference: Contact conference leaders to tell them you're exploring their field and will be at the conference. Arrange to meet with them, and ask them which seminars you should definitely attend, and could they introduce you to people you ought to meet.

At least a week before the conference: If you're net-working in a new field, you may not want to use your current business card. Instead, get inexpensive business cards printed up with your name, contact information, and a quote if you like. (This is a good idea whether or not you're attending a conference.)

Right before the conference: Bring a spiral notebook, which will be your "Interest/Idea Journal." Write at the top of the first page, "This sounds interesting. . . " Write brief notes about whatever at the conference catches your interest. Only use it for this purpose, and after the conference you'll be able to examine your notes and look for themes or specific ideas worth following up on. It's really a right-brain journal, since you're only capturing what sparks your interest. (This exercise is important whether or not you're at a conference. If you're using a journal as you read this book, flip it over and start your "Interest/Idea Journal" from the back of the notebook. You can use a highlighter to color the outside edges of the pages dedicated to noting ideas that spark your interest to keep it separate from the rest of the journal.)

At the conference:

- Plan to stay in touch with, and network with, people you like, not with people you are uncomfortable with but who you think would be important for your career. Gather cards and write a note on every card so you'll know why that person interested you, and anything else that will refresh your memory after the conference. Don't assume you'll remember specifics. Conferences are hectic and you'll meet too many people to remember even important details.

- Be helpful to those you meet if you have something to offer them. Make a note of what you can do to help them, and get in touch with them after the conference.

- You're not there to ask for favors. It's appropriate to feel grateful for any help you receive. But take the attitude that you're there to interact with people who share your passionate interest in the field. Others who also have a passion for their work will want to help you learn about the field, and you'll be able to connect with like-minded people with whom you can network after the event is over.

After the conference: Make sure you follow up with those people you offered to contact.

E-mail from Julie

Subj: Getting ready for the conference
From: julie@bigcompany.com

Dear Leslie,

Okay, I have my networking cards, my Interest/Idea Journal, and the program for the conference and I'm playing phone tag with the conference coordinators.

What else do I do once I'm there?

Best,

Julie

Dear Julie:

Great work! Once you're there, stay focused on these three things (unless you get pulled in a great new direction):

1. Research what kind of work mediators are doing.

2. Research what products or services clients are motivated (and able) to buy.

3. Look for what *your* niche could be.

The Inner Critic

The inner critic is one of the most dangerous threats to experimenting with a new idea. The "inner critic" is our inner voice that tells us that our ideas are no good, that our plans are too risky and that we should be very worried about all of the negative consequences that could happen if we try to improve our lives.

It can come when you get the Visa bill in the mail that includes the fee for an art course you signed up for. Your inner critic might say, "You can't afford that. You can't even draw! Maybe other people can spend that kind of money on a dream, but you can't."

Or it may come when you sit down to write a press release for a project you've always wanted to do. This time it might say, "Who's going to want to hear about that?! News reporters have more important things to do than to read about your workshop."

Our inner critic is not the same as our conscience. Our conscience helps us to develop good character by letting us know when we're about to do something wrong or hurtful. That's a good thing. Our inner critic is a harsh inner judge who is never happy—you can't please it, even though it makes you think that if you were just good enough you could.

So how do you override the inner critic? It's very clever, so you have to know when you're dealing with it so you can keep it in its place. They're like the "agents" in the movie *The Matrix* who were out to destroy the authentic people, but were disguised as upstanding citizens. If you think you might be dealing with your inner critic, ask yourself the following questions:

- Do I feel defeated before I even start this activity?
- Is my mind full of reasons this *won't* work, but not one *positive* idea?

- Do I feel stupid, inadequate or incompetent?

If you answered yes to any of these questions, you're dealing with your inner critic. And it's not trying to help you by preventing you from *embarrassing* yourself. It's trying to prevent you from *becoming* yourself. We think we have to accept our inner critic. But have you ever felt guilty when you put your feet on the coffee table or when you eat in bed? You might have laughed and said to yourself, I'm forty-three years old, I can eat in bed if I want!

We don't have to put up with our inner critic, either. Just because it's a familiar voice doesn't mean we have to let it boss us around. It's an element of our dark side and only serves a destructive function. It might sound simplistic to "just say no" to your inner critic, but starving it and stopping it from building up any momentum is the best way I know to defeat it before it makes us feel defeated.

What to Do?

- Pay attention to your basic needs. Get plenty of sleep, try to maintain an even-temperedness and inner calm, eat a balanced diet and exercise a little every day. (This reminds me of the wise twelve-step program warning that says, "Don't get too tired, too angry, or too hungry.")
- It's okay to notice what you're feeling, but you don't have to act on that feeling.
- Try to take the "witness" perspective of observing your feelings.
- Always look for the higher truth. Distance yourself from the negative thoughts and do something to put you in a higher, creative frame of mind.
- Don't give in to your inner critic!

If you know what the inner critic sounds like and feels like, and you can take a step back to the witness position, you can then confidently and calmly ignore your inner critic.

You've Got a Solid Foundation

You've drafted your Mission Statement, your Family & Personal Goals and Guideposts, and your Career & Business Goals and Guideposts. And you may have a "good enough starting point"[25] for your career/business path, and guideposts that tell you what you need to do and to avoid.

The next chapter will help you uncover the conflicts between your various needs, goals and guideposts. These conflicts cause an incredible amount of frustration, and can stay hidden for a very long time.

> *I know it sounds hokey, but I think it was life changing. I now work with someone who's helping me plan my financial future-something I would never have considered prior to this process. Planning is a good thing!*
>
> *Rather than feeling hemmed in by "THE PLAN," I am excited about the implementation and am enjoying putting the pieces together—which is much easier when you have a plan. Before, there was a lot of, "Well, I'll try this and see how it flies."*

---

[25] *I borrow the phrase "good enough" from D.W. Winnicott, who wrote about "good enough mothering." There's no perfect mother, and if there was, her baby would be missing the normal frustrations needed to develop properly. But the good-enough mother doesn't allow her baby to be completely overwhelmed and is basically responsive and loving. Similarly, there is no ideal job out there for you. But if you pick a starting point with potential that allows you to express your calling in some way, you'll evolve along with it and eventually come across a great opportunity that will be the right fit for you.*

The most important thing to me is that my business plan be an honest representation of me and my company. I looked at a couple of other business plans written by (or for) pet-dog trainers, and they were devoid of personality.

My plan is now professional and complete, and at the same time, it has a lot of me in there! I feel that if you read my plan you get a real sense of what Canine's Best Behavior is all about.

—Elaine Allison

CHAPTER SEVEN

Your Synergy Plan Allows You to Identify and Resolve Hidden Conflicts

*"I started the school because I wanted
to make sure our kids had the right education.
The irony was that because of my efforts,
they didn't have the best homelife
during that time."*

— Debi Corso, Founder
Seven Peaks Elementary School

I think I surprised Michelle, an ambitious entrepreneur who came to my office for feedback on her business plan. Her plan included the financial goal of growing her business until it grossed fifty million dollars annually within five years. We met at the height of the tech boom, and Michelle had developed a new technology for computer networking and was ready to bring her product into a ripe market. But when she asked for advice on growing her business according to this goal, my response surprised her. She came in expecting a formula for selling a certain number of units through particular distribution channels. Instead we talked about her family life.

"My family is really important to me. My son is eleven years old and my daughter is seven. But I've always dreamed of owning my own business."

Hidden conflicts between your various values, and between your intentions and your behavior, cause you to act in ways that don't contribute to your true goals, and often sabotage those very goals.

"But why do you want to grow your business so fast? From what you've described in your plan, you'll have to work at least six days, and seventy to eighty hours a week, to reach your goal. Are you sure you want to do that?"

Michelle had simply assumed that she could have a family and personal life while growing her business. However, her personal and family goals, which were truly important to her, were completely inconsistent with her business goals. She needed a plan that included all three aspects of her life.

Hidden Conflicts Undermine Your Most Cherished Goals

How can intelligent, caring women striving toward an admirable goal neglect the people they aim to nurture, including themselves? It may seem counterintuitive, but it's actually quite easy to explain. Hidden conflicts between your various values, and between your intentions and your behavior, cause you to act in ways that don't contribute to your true goals, and often sabotage those very goals. This chapter will show you, step by step, how to first identify and then resolve the hidden conflicts that may already be undermining your best intentions.

There are several types of hidden conflicts. Here are some common ones:

- When your vision is out of touch with reality
- When your career & business goals and guideposts sabotage your family's needs
- When your family's needs and guideposts sabotage your personal needs

You may think of others that are meaningful to you.

Is Your Vision in Touch with Reality?

When you created your Mission Statement in the previous chapter, I asked you to avoid including a specific job title. Your mission also shouldn't reflect short-term limitations. Your Mission Statement is as much about *who you are* as it is about *what you do*.

When you're trying to stay focused on your key values, you don't want temporary circumstances to limit your view. Some people overcompensate in this area by creating a Mission Statement that doesn't take reality into consideration at all. Your mission should be based on who you truly are, not who you wish to be (if that isn't your true self).

Take another look now at your Mission Statement. If it's just beyond your current reach, but realistic as a long-term and all-encompassing goal, then you've nailed it! If it's more wishful thinking then realistic, go back now and make some changes.

The ideal for eating right is to find a healthy diet you can follow for life, not one that leaves you feeling deprived, or one that is so time-consuming that you rarely use it. Similarly, you need to create a Synergy Plan that leads to a schedule, pace and field of endeavor that you can live with throughout your career.

Are Your Career & Business Goals Sabotaging Your Family's Needs?

This is the hidden conflict that I see most often with entrepreneurs. But it can easily get in the way of any ambitious career-woman. Ask yourself if you feel that *both* your business and family life are suffering. Do you feel at a loss about how to improve both situations? Do you make matters worse by redoubling your efforts at work while raising your expectations of how you'll interact with your family?

In the past when I didn't feel I was achieving my goals, I'd set new goals that were often more daunting than the ones I was falling short of. When I put in even more effort at work, I exhausted myself physically, mentally and spiritually. And, I wasn't getting much additional work done! I made mental errors, which made me spend even more time to clean up the mess.

If you raise your expectations of how you'll relate to your family while you're adding goals and targets to reach at work, you're increasing the gap between what you expect and what actually happens. This increasing gap leads to the feeling that you're failing more than ever.

Are Your Family's Needs and Guidelines Sabotaging Your Personal Needs?

Just as your business or career plans can conflict with family goals and needs, your personal needs can easily conflict with those of your family. For example, if you regularly put your family's needs before your own, you might feel depleted and deprived. You may neglect exercising as much as you'd like, or you may not take the time and energy to improve your diet. You may rarely have time to read or to relax in a hot bath.

You can only neglect your own needs and aspirations for so long before you run out of fuel. This is one way to lose your passion for life and get in the habit of running on "fumes."

It's easier than it sounds to act in conflict with our root values. It usually happens when our focus is on the surface so that we don't notice the deeper value buried below. Let's say you care about being available to your kids. One of the things you try to do is to be home when your children get home from school, but your boss schedules late meetings at least once a week. If you explore how your behavior seems to clash with your core value of being available to your kids, you may find that you also value being seen as a "good girl" at work, and that you value staying away from conflict. By examining your behavior, you can learn about your hidden values or fears, and you can pick out the ones that get in the way of your core values and change them.

The next section will show you how to spot conflicting values and sort out which you want to live by, and which are undermining achieving success on your terms.

What Are Your Conflicts?

Do you have conflicts in these important aspects of your life? Perhaps all three (career, family, and personal goals and needs) are a source of conflict for you. Or there may be other areas you've identified that worry you and create stress and tension in your life. For example, not having the time or energy to devote to religious or spiritual practice can create stress for many of us.

You Can Resolve Conflicts Between Business, Family, and Personal Goals and Guideposts

This chapter's worksheet, Goal Conflicts & Resolutions, lets you figure out how to rethink strategies or goals that threaten to sabotage specific goals or even your overall mission. If you're an entrepreneur and have a business plan, you have at least some idea of how much time and energy you'll need to follow that plan. But because most business plans are written without regard for even the most basic family and personal goals, typical business plans are likely to achieve success only at the expense of sacrificing "non-business" goals. If you don't have a business plan (and many small business owners don't) or if you work for someone else, you're going to be even *less* likely to see the potential conflicts and mine-fields between your career, family and personal goals.

Most clients I've worked with have never explicitly spelled out their personal and family goals and guideposts. And some career women don't even have a family calendar where they post important dates and events for all family members to see. After using the Synergy Planning process, you may feel torn between different goals at times, but you won't miss out on what means the most to you.

Trail Marker: *A great deal of stress is due to acting in ways which are inconsistent with our values. The more our actions are consistent with our values, the less stressed we'll feel.*

With your Mission Statement, Family & Personal Goals and Guideposts, and Career & Business Goals and Guideposts Worksheets (found in chapter 6) in front of you, approach the worksheet on the next page with an open mind, ready to brainstorm as many possible solutions as you can. If you open your mind to as many options as you can, you maximize your chances of finding the right path for you and your family.

Synergy Plan℠ Worksheet:
Goal Conflicts & Resolutions *(Sample)*

STEP ONE: List your priorities here (use previous worksheets on pages 161, 167, 173 if you've filled them out)

Family: Be home when kids get home from school; keep my focus on them in the afternoon and evening.

Personal: Take time for myself (½ hour a day) without feeling guilty.

Career: Learn to delegate so I can be more efficient at work; let others do their part *their* way; find a mentor to help me learn this skill.

STEP TWO: Consider what could be conflicting with each of these priorities.

Family: I'm either not home due to work, chores or errands; or when I'm home it's hard to stay focused on the kids when I can get distracted by housework. I need to explore whether I feel like I'm "goofing off" if I'm having fun with the kids; and I'd like to find a way to avoid getting distracted by dishes in the sink, etc., when it's time to be with the kids.

Personal: I feel a pull to fill my downtime with activities. I need to allow myself to have quiet time when I'm not doing anything, and realize that it's productive.

Career: I feel that I need to be on top of every detail so that I can control the outcome; I like people to report to me so that the end result turns out exactly the way I envision it.

Synergy Plan℠ Worksheet:
Goal Conflicts & Resolutions *(Blank)*

Step One: List your priorities here (use previous worksheets on pages 161, 167, 173 if you've filled them out)

Family: _____

_____

_____

Personal: _____

_____

_____

Career: _____

_____

_____

Step Two: Consider what could be conflicting with each of these priorities.

Family: _____

_____

_____

Personal: _____

_____

_____

Career: _____

_____

_____

Step Three: What needs to be done, reviewed, and/or discussed to resolve each conflict listed above? Be specific. How might you be allowing weaknesses or lower level priorities to sabotage acting on your best intentions? (For example: wanting to avoid conflict, needing recognition, wanting to be perceived as a hard worker, needing to be in control of every detail of a project.) Don't forget to mention who else needs to be involved in the solution.

a) _____

_____

b) _____

_____

c) _____

_____

d) _____

_____

Step Four: List the steps you'll take to resolve these conflicts. Note beginning and ending dates, if they apply.

Action	Begin Date	Deadline
1)		
2)		
3)		

BOTTOM LINE: (Sum up the most important lesson you need to learn from this worksheet so you can quickly and easily remind yourself what's the bottom line.)

_____

_____

How will you resolve the conflicts at home? Will you schedule all your work and chores so they're completed when your children get home from school? Will you try to greet your kids by asking how their day was and then listening instead of running down a mental checklist of questions about homework, test scores, and upcoming activities?

What about in your personal life? How will you address your need for a little time each day for yourself? Can you find a reliable mother's helper so you can get half an hour a few times a week so you can put on your yoga video in the den? Can you swap child care with a trusted friend or relative one day a week? Can your spouse keep an eye on the kids for a little while each weekend so you can get out of the house?

How will you resolve your conflicts at work? Will you call a meeting to explain to people that you want them to take on the project as if it were their own? Or will you privately encourage each coworker to make important decisions when they turn to you for guidance, and support their (good) ideas even when they're different than yours?

Is there anyone else who needs to be involved in these decisions? Is there anyone else who may be able to give you objective feedback, if needed? Do you have a mentor you can ask? Is it time to look for such a person?

What's Hiding Behind Your Blind Spots?

Are there blind spots that get in the way as you try to act on your values? Many blind spots are a result of our emotional attachments to expectations, people, and/or material possessions.

I had a huge blind spot. After I realized that my dream of opening a Parenting Center wasn't realistic (as I discussed in chapter 6),

I started up Parent Support Services. It eventually became a consulting firm, and I had control over my schedule and did all the work myself. But when I first started it up, I was working on a pilot project that I hoped would lead to offering parenting support services throughout the state of California through one of the largest managed health care companies in the country. I formed a partnership with a trusted friend, started writing my business plan and set my sights on hiring staff to fulfill my end of the deal.

I was coming off of being burned out from working too intensely, and neglecting my family and personal life. And I would have thrown myself into an even worse dilemma if that pilot project had worked out. But my blind spot prevented me from becoming inwardly mobile and focused me instead on growing the biggest, most outwardly successful business I could.

I realize now that striving for outward success was my way to compensate for not feeling worthwhile just for being myself—my true self. I thought that I was special if I did something special. Now, when I think about my attitude toward my self-worth, I think, "If I'm created in God's image, and if my soul is the Divine spark within me, then I can tune into that spark that is already infinitely valuable. And if I think and act and relate to others from the Divine part of me, I'll share that value in some small way."

> *Eternity is a dimension of here and now.*
> *The divine lives within you.*
> *Live from your own center.*[26]
>
> — JOSEPH CAMPBELL

---

[26] Diane K. Osbon, ed. *Reflections on the Art of Living: A Joseph Campbell Companion.* New York: Harper Collins, 1991. p. 21.

If you have a calling to run a large company, and you don't have family obligations that get in the way, do it as part of your higher calling. But I would have put myself right back on the hamster wheel again. I would have had to work at least sixty hours a week (and more if I hadn't had a partner), I would have had to eventually train dozens of staff members, and would have had to supervise the whole program and handle clinical crises and staff issues. I would have been doing something I thought was helpful, but I would not have been following my calling, which is what led me to become burned out in the first place. For someone who prefers being home every evening and weekend, doesn't like to travel much and hates a hectic schedule, I was a perfect example of why regular business planning methods, which help us plan how to make our *business* thrive but not make *us* thrive, can get us completely off our unique paths.

Not the Same as a New Year's Resolution

How will you address the challenges that interfere with your resolve to stay focused on your mission? Making a commitment to living a more meaningful and inwardly mobile life is a shift in your whole outlook. It's very different from making a New Year's resolution, for example. Typically, resolutions address superficial aspects of life, like habits. If you've ever decided to quit smoking, or to go to the gym more often, or to give up Chunky Monkey ice cream, you know that a resolution is half wish and half willpower. Neither is strong enough to last until President's Day, unless something happened to deepen your resolve and shift your consciousness. If you'd had a heart attack in November, for example, your resolution to exercise regularly might last for the rest of your life. It's no longer just a matter of willpower. A deeper shift took place inside of you.

That's the kind of shift we need to make. This shift requires using our burnout as a wake-up call to realize that our life is off-track, and to be motivated by the desperate feeling that we can't go on in the wrong direction any longer, getting further from expressing our true self until we forever lose the chance to become who we really are.

Once we have that realization, and fully commit ourselves to pursuing our true path, we may need to clarify our roles at work or at home to clear the course ahead of us. Once *we're* clear about what living by our values looks like in our day-to-day life, we can start to communicate the specifics to others, as appropriate.

Communicating Your Values to Others

The more clear you are about your values, the more clearly you'll communicate them to others. If you find yourself feeling defensive or overly concerned that others won't respect your boundaries that protect these essential values, you may not be clear in your *own* mind about the importance of these values to your well-being. A client of mine, Joan, was afraid that once she decided to put time with her family and her own well-being above working overtime, her boss wouldn't take her seriously. The first couple of times that she turned down assignments her boss *was* actually surprised, which Joan took as validation of her fears. But when Joan and I worked on her resistance to changing her behavior, she started noticing how much deeper and more fun her relationships at home were now that she was around more. She saw more clearly that pleasing others at work, if she *was* even pleasing others by neglecting her family, wasn't worth giving up being a more active family member. And "miraculously" her boss and co-workers didn't question her motives anymore. In fact, some of them followed her example.

Getting Support from Your Employer

Although the business case for allowing employees to control their schedules and take time for family commitments has been made many times over, too many employers still cling to old standards of rigid schedules and plenty of "face time."

If you're able to understand your company's needs and priorities, as well as those specific to your boss (and her boss), you'll be able to make a convincing and powerful presentation of your ideas for ensuring that these corporate needs get met. This professional approach works well with most employers. There are exceptions, and unfortunately even though you may have presented a strong case for a more flexible situation, some supervisors just can't grasp that you've successfully answered their objections.

Try not to feel defensive or victimized. And if you find yourself taking their response personally, try your best to recognize your reaction and detach yourself from those feelings. Then be as objective as you can about whether there's a chance to get what you need at that particular job, if you can transfer to another position or if you have to look elsewhere for employment. You're in a search for the truth, not in a contest to win or lose. If you can convey this to your boss and coworkers, and give them the chance to share that search, they may cooperate with you to find a solution that meets everyone's needs.

- A 1997 AT&T survey of active telecommuters revealed that 36 percent would quit or find another home-based job if their employer decided they could no longer work at home.

- A similar study by the Families and Work Institute revealed that more than one-third (35 percent) of employees with children under the age of 15 say they would change jobs if they found one offering more flexible work arrangements.

- In an AT&T-sponsored survey of Fortune 1000 telemanagers, 58 percent reported increased worker productivity.

- The state of California's telecommuting pilot program measured productivity increases of 10 percent to 30 percent, and American Express tallied a 20 percent productivity gain for off-site call center employees.

- A facilities manager at Lucent Technologies estimates that for every dollar spent setting up a home office, the company saves two dollars in real estate expenses.

- According to the 1996 Unscheduled Absence Survey by CCH Inc., absenteeism costs U.S. companies $603 per employee per year. The National Safety Council says that on an average workday, one million employees are absent from work because of stress-related problems.

- By contrast, telecommuters can work from home when a minor illness or sick child keeps them from the office. Unisys found that its telecommuters take 33 percent less sick leave than other workers. Teleworkers at Holland America Westours take two fewer days off per year than their office colleagues.[27]

---

[27] June Langhoff. "A Telemanager's Index: The Definitive Roundup of Telecommuting Statistics." Home Office Computing, April, 1999. www.findarticles.com/cf_0/m1563/4_17/54256828/print.jhtml

I'm very optimistic about the future of job-sharing and other flexible work arrangements. Young people entering the workforce now expect to have a life outside of work. They don't see the logic behind sacrificing their goals for their company, especially since staying at one company for life is no longer a desired goal, nor a possibility in most cases. Their expectations and approach to their career has hastened the changes that the baby boomer generation initiated but had merely hoped for (in most cases), not demanded.

Communicating with Your Clients

Let's say you've decided that you won't travel more than three days in any month in order to have more family time and feel less stressed. But a client wants you to do a customer service training for multiple out-of-state branch offices. You can tell that this project is going to require you to spend several weeks out of town. As you mull over how to explain that you only travel three days in any month, you start to worry that this client will take her business elsewhere, and that you'll not only lose the new training opportunity, but the whole account.

If you focus on the exact number of days you're available for travel, you'll lose sight of why this is so important to you and you'll only express the rule to the client. You'll sound rigid, or worse, you may give the impression that you're not willing to do what's needed to solve your client's business problems.

But if you focus on your values and remember why you established this rule in the first place (to be home with family as much as possible), your client will pick up on your commitment to your family. You'll communicate that there's a principle and larger context causing you to turn down the project, and that this isn't merely an arbitrary decision. Your client may even admire your ability to set limits for the sake of family and personal commitments. Or you may find out that this client doesn't expect you to have a life or even any other clients besides her.

You can avoid a lot of unpleasant problems with clients by evaluating if there's a good match early in the relationship. The response you get when sharing your availability with prospects and new clients is only one way to judge if there's a good or bad fit. But you can learn a lot about others by how they react to your boundaries.

Explaining to Clients That You Work from Home

Even if you don't work from home full time, you may do some telecommuting, or simply return some calls to clients from your home. When the first wave of businesspeople began working from home, it was done with a great deal of secrecy. They panicked if their dog barked, their baby cried or the neighbor's gardeners used a leaf blower while they were on the phone with a client. It wasn't considered professional to work from home. A lot has changed since then. For most businesspeople, working from home and being an involved parent no longer implies that you're less professional. Work-at-home professionals are even envied by those who face long commutes and don't have the chance to have breakfast with their children or spouse.

Still, most of your clients don't need to know whether you work out of your home, and I don't think you should tell all of them. Your clients simply want you to get their job done without inconveniencing them.

E-mail from Julie

Subj: Scheduling
From: julie@bigcompany.com

Hi Leslie,

I was really concerned about my schedule, as you know. I can't drop Mark off at school until 8 A.M. at the earliest, which means the soonest I can get into the city is 9 A.M. That's a big problem when a client asks me to deliver a workshop beginning at 9 A.M.—not enough time for transportation, let alone set-up.

But to my great (and ongoing) surprise, every time I've explained this to a client, they are lovely about it, easily moving the start time to accommodate me. So far, I've had to ask clients to shift things just a little, and I try to compensate by exceeding their expectation in terms of delivery and the final product.

I know you told me this would work out, but to be honest, I wasn't sure that it would. This is a huge relief.

Best,
Julie

Communicating with Your Employees

If you have employees, they deserve the same level of consideration as your clients. Only you can determine how much of yourself to share with them, but the same guidelines apply. The clearer you are on the importance of your values, the more matter-of-fact and the less defensive you'll sound. My experience coaching small-business owners has taught me that employers who tout family values but who criticize employees for not putting in enough "face time," or who work excessive hours themselves, are leading by their poor example. The fact that they pay lip service to family values causes even *lower* levels of morale than if they were honest and said that a one-dimensional workaholic employee with no outside "distractions" is most likely to succeed in their company. Companies who put on a show about being "family friendly" but don't back it up with action kill morale with their hypocrisy.

Communicating with Your Family

Most of these principles hold true when it comes to talking to your spouse about your personal goals and needs. But it's even harder to stay objective and conduct the search for the truth I've been describing when it's your husband and not your boss whom you want to understand your point of view. Fortunately, your husband is likely to share your concern for meeting your family's needs even if you have different ideas about how to do so. Assuming that your aim is to do the right thing for your family, your husband will probably be a valuable brainstorming partner and source of moral support.

First, get clear on *why* you are invested in a certain goal. Then explain your position directly and calmly. If your husband has an objection, hear him out. He may care more than you think about a particular issue. We can forget how radical even small changes seemed to us when they were new ideas. If you are used to the changes already, but are just now sharing them with your spouse, let him get used to them at his own pace.

If your husband is completely unsupportive of anything you do to continue your personal growth or to better meet your children's needs, you are in an unhealthy relationship. This topic is worthy of another book, and I won't try to fully cover it here. We choose our spouse based on both conscious and subconscious needs. If you've previously been afraid of change and your top priority was to find security, you probably found a man who resists change and wants to keep the status quo. You can't expect him to now support your new demands without some work on both your parts.

One of my clients, Sheila, found herself in a similar dilemma. She married young, was anxious to escape the strong gravitational pull of her controlling parents, and found a man who was good at making her feel secure. Steve was comfortable being in charge, helped her stand up to her parents and was very caring to her. After twelve years of marriage, though, she was ready to take charge of her own life. This was a new concept not just to him, but to the relationship. Sheila didn't realize that she had helped create what was now restricting her progress.

It took some marital therapy, but they were both able to see that Sheila was trying to grow, not to leave Steve behind, and Steve was willing to move out of his comfort zone of being in charge for the good of both his wife and their marriage.

Not all couples are able to make these changes, and bad marriages will get worse the more you get in touch with your true self. But the more clear you are about what you're striving for, and the less you feel that everyone is out to stop you and that you have to fight for survival, the more likely you and your husband are to work together toward a solution that makes sense.

Don't fall back on "that's just how I decided to do it" if you want anyone else to understand your values and priorities, and get behind them. If your husband hasn't been aware of all of the internal changes you've been going through, share some of them with him. He'll probably be more willing to make the effort to understand your needs.

When you and your husband have discussed how your new career, family and personal goals and guidelines will affect your home life, explain to your children (if you have any) what this will mean to them. If their eyes glaze over at a certain point, you've probably gone into too much detail. Just tell them enough so that they know it's okay to talk to you about it when they have more questions. And if your family is used to broken promises about spending more time with them, just make the changes and don't talk much about it. It will take some time to win back their trust that you really do intend to be around more.

Not Just Problem Solving

Most of us find it easier to approach our values conflicts in the same way we would any other business or career problem—in a practical way. When we think about changing our goals as a practical problem to solve, we don't have to feel the weight of a moral dilemma. But if our goals are based on our values, that means that by weaseling out of the moral dilemma, we're putting our values on the same plane as any other practical problem, like which brand of computer to buy. Once we get used to first clarifying our values and *then* working out the details, the process starts to feel very natural. As I pointed out earlier, a great deal of unnecessary stress is caused downstream by acting in a way that isn't consistent with our values at the top of the stream.

An Ongoing Job

Developing a Synergy Plan is only the beginning of an ongoing process. The goal is not only to clarify your goals and priorities and get them down on paper. Creating your plan does force you to get focused, clear up conflicting goals and to spell out how to move forward. But, because of the constantly changing relationship between the various aspects of your life, and the fact that living a balanced life is an ongoing challenge, (especially if you have both family responsibilities and a career), your work will never be "done" in the conventional sense. If you complete the worksheets just to check them off your to-do list and file them away, you'll miss the opportunity to gain so much more from all the work you're doing now.

There are a lot of ways to continue to reap the benefits of creating your Synergy Plan. One way is to schedule time, monthly at first, then quarterly, to review your worksheets and related materials. Be sure to include any key colleagues, or any staff members, in these review meetings. If you work by yourself, review your materials with a friend or colleague. (Ideally, you can do the worksheets and other planning materials, and the reviews, together at regular intervals.) Revise your plan, then discuss the changes with your partner, as well as any new insights you've had. Let her do the same with you.

Another idea is to post your Mission Statement in plain view as a daily reminder of why you do what you do. It can also help to keep your focus on that deeper theme when your mind is pulled to the surface to your to-do list, or how to get the next sale. Brainstorm ways to maintain your balance and calmness when you're having a hectic day.

I'd love to hear from you about how you are getting the most return on your investment from the Synergy Plan materials in this book. Write, fax or e-mail me with a description of how you've gotten results from these materials, or suggestions you have to make them more useful. My contact information, including my Web site address, is at the end of the book on page 307.

Many parents tell me, as they describe the ongoing challenges of raising their children, that as soon as they finally understand their child's *current* developmental stage, it changes. Your child's fast-changing, ongoing progress is similar to both your own personal growth process, and that of your career path. That means that you can't base your Synergy Plan on the tempting fantasy of some unchanging period of stability in your business or career. It's a tool that's useful only to the extent that you use it while you're moving forward on your path.

Most of us want life to hold still for a while so we can analyze it, make sense of it and have some predictability to our existence. You may think that this is a matter of personal preference, but it's a hardwired tendency that goes back to our earliest origins. Part of early mankind's survival depended on knowing what to expect and not encountering too many surprises. You may personally enjoy being surprised, or feel bored if you're not constantly challenged by something new. This is because we all count on life being fairly predictable, and only within the safety of that stability can we appreciate some chaos to spice things up a little.

The truth is that it goes against our deep brain structure to expect and enjoy ongoing, unpredictable change that is beyond our control. So it's not out of laziness that even those of us who are really dedicated to thinking through how we want to live and work put our career or business plans on the shelf. We want to feel that we've solved that problem, put it behind us and can now tackle something new. One way I try to combat this natural tendency in my clients, in addition to its usefulness as a marketing tool, is to send reminder faxes, e-mail or postcards on a regular basis to remind them to review and revise their Synergy Plans.

Prioritize

One of the immediate benefits you should realize in completing the worksheets is a feeling of being focused and clear about what's important to you. Your Mission Statement was the first step. You spelled out the big picture of what you hope to accomplish, how that relates to the work you do, and included important family responsibilities and personal goals. You may have also included a reference to how you'll accomplish your mission.

The Family & Personal Goals and Guideposts and Career & Business Goals and Guideposts or worksheets are the next steps. Once you're clear on the overall mission, your specific goals and guidelines will tell you how to get there and help you know when you're veering off course. No matter how specific and realistic your goals are, if they don't reflect your deeper mission, they won't help and could get in the way. Let your mission set the course and give you some clue as to what type of journey you'll be taking. The specific Career & Business, Family & Personal Guideposts you've begun drafting in chapter 6, and the concrete steps you'll spell out in chapter 8, will put those intentions into action.

Why Plan at All?

Why should we make specific plans in such detail, if we can't determine where our career path should go from our limited perspective? It's true, we can't plan every detail of our lives. But the point is, if we put ourselves on a rewarding, meaningful path, we'll expose ourselves to opportunities consistent with our values and needs. Staying on the right path also becomes a good habit, reinforced with each positive experience of developing a relationship with our true selves. Chapter 8 explores this paradox in more detail. We need to, and can, plan some of our activities. But we still have to admit that very often the most rewarding or interesting aspects of our lives are those we could not have planned nor even anticipated. "The Path Is the Goal" method of planning addresses both sides of this apparent paradox.

To help you get focused and stay focused in a realistic way, your Synergy Plan should include no more than two or three top priorities. And among those priorities, I recommend that you set one value or priority that *cannot* be compromised. Use that essential priority as a measuring stick. Hold up all opportunities against it. This gives you a good idea of which opportunities to accept, reject or merely put on hold.

Most of us judge an opportunity based on its attractiveness in some superficial way. For example, you might approach a decision to accept a promotion based on how much money is offered, if it will sound impressive to family and friends, or if you're bored with your current situation and a new opportunity would give you a change of scenery. *Instead, think of each possibility as an opportunity to stay on your chosen path, or to stray from what you really want and need to accomplish.* This process clarifies what might be a much tougher decision, and helps you make the choice based on what's most important to you.

Stay Focused Every Day

I've discussed how to consciously plan for the future in order to live according to your most important values and priorities. But what about planning day-to-day activities? Here are some ways to make sure you take care of what's most important every day:

- Review what needs to be done daily, and choose no more than two or three priorities. I strongly recommend one top priority item per day.
- If you still can't seem to stay focused and often feel frazzled, keep a log of your time for a few days and pay attention to what interrupts you as you're working on high-priority items. You have to be honest and detailed, or don't bother with this method.

I tried keeping a log like this once, with surprising results. I consider myself to be very focused and productive, so it was a shock to discover that even when I was working on something I considered very important, if the phone rang and the caller asked me to do something else, I immediately shifted my focus from what I needed to accomplish and got right to work on that much less important task. Prior to my logging experiment, if you'd asked me how I spent my workday, I had no clue that I lost my focus so easily. I'm now much humbler, and more productive. If after a few days of log-keeping you don't see a pattern in what takes you off task, you're either not looking hard enough, or the self-consciousness has put you on your best behavior.

Trail Marker: *Set aside an hour each day for top priority activities. Only work on those activities during that time.*

Use an Interest/Idea Journal

If you're like me, and have "earth-shattering" ideas for new projects distracting you on a daily basis, you won't stay focused on what needs to get done. You can only do one major special project every six months, unless you have extra staff members only for that purpose. Since most of us don't have that luxury, consider starting an "Interest/Idea Journal." Enter ideas for projects, goals, ways to collaborate with colleagues and any other specifics for new projects that you don't have the time, energy or funds for right now. Review it regularly to weed out those ideas that weren't so earth-shattering after all, and to make sure you don't forget about that truly wonderful idea you should make time for. Your scheduled sabbatical is a great time to review your Interest/Idea Journal.

 Trail Marker: *Start a section of your journal for ideas that don't fit into your current strategic plan but are worth saving.*

Take a Sabbatical

Take two days off every six months to review your Synergy Plan, and to keep a perspective on your career or business. (If you can, take a week off. Often, the first couple of days of a sabbatical are spent thinking about what is going on at the office. When you know you have a week off, you can clear your mind of your day-to-day tasks that much more, and focus on the big picture more effectively.)

- Schedule your sabbatical now.
- Schedule important items around that week (such as billing and other important tasks).
- Leave an outgoing message on your voice mail that calls will be returned the following week (and that only urgent calls will be returned immediately).

If you're an entrepreneur, consider using a professional strategic planner or coach at first. Share the cost with other small-business owners if necessary. Although you won't spend the whole time on your business in a small group, you'll learn from others' experiences and develop a great support system. It's easier to approach an issue objectively when you're listening to someone else discussing a problem that you're also concerned about. And even if you typically excel at *initiating* new projects, you may not be as skilled at *following through* on each necessary step. Having someone to hold you accountable for important details and deadlines can make a big difference. They can also help you determine which details are important, and which to delegate or eliminate— another weak spot for many of us.

Get Out of the Office

Do you get lost in all of the things that need to be organized, filed or written, or seduced by the most addictive vice of all: checking your e-mail? Here are some strategies to help you get out of the office and transition into not working:

- Set your watch or computer alarm for the time you want to leave.

- Have a plan to do something else after work.
  - –Exercise works well, because it provides a clear transition that gets you out of the office and keeps your mind off work.
  - –Schedule an activity with your family.
  - –Take a hot bath.
  - –Read for pleasure.

If you've been around young children, you know that you can't interrupt them while they're involved in one activity and expect them to immediately shift their focus to another. They need time to transition. That's why most parents use a bedtime ritual to help with one of the hardest transitions—from being awake and having fun with the family to being alone and falling asleep. So think about how you can allow yourself some time to transition out of work mode.

I'm a huge sports fan, so when there's a sporting event that I want to watch, I plan to be out of the office in time to work out in front of the television. This works especially well for me during hockey season.

If you can't yet imagine leaving the office early without feeling like you're playing hooky, remember that if you start your day by working on your top priority item(s), they'll probably be completed by the end of your work day. This makes it easier to leave the office, because you're not leaving essential items undone.

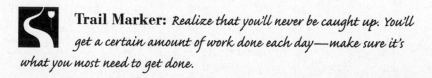 **Trail Marker:** *Realize that you'll never be caught up. You'll get a certain amount of work done each day—make sure it's what you most need to get done.*

Look at How You Use Time in a New Light

It's possible to change the way you think about, and make use of, your time. Sally, president of a small health services company in Southern California, has discovered a way to focus on priorities, not hours. She explains:

> I'm trying to work more effectively, not work harder. I try to have a laser focus on high priorities. With this focus, I can work less than eight hours a day and still have a successful business. At first I couldn't imagine how I could take the time off I needed for my family. In the beginning I felt a little strange leaving work to pick up my son at 3:30 P.M., but once I saw the effectiveness of working smarter, the anxiety of leaving work "early" vanished. I'm at the point now where I don't even see a day in terms of time. I look at what is on my priority list to grow this business today. If I can do this in four hours, fine. Some days it may take more than that, but at least now I know the difference.

Try a Meditation Exercise

Does the word meditation remind you of sitting uncomfortably and vainly struggling to clear your mind of a steady stream of thoughts about what needs to get done until it's time to get back to your real life? Meditation can help you stay focused or relax, but it's not just another "technique" to make you more productive.

If you want to successfully meditate, you have to commit to doing it every day. Start out by meditating first thing in the morning, so you won't forget or get too busy later in the day. Sit in a quiet place, with good posture, for ten to fifteen minutes, with the goal of clearing your mind, asking for guidance and listening to a wiser part of yourself—one that is not so caught up in the day-to-day conflicts, struggles and pressures of life. There are many ways to meditate, and many reasons to do so. Some meditation books for beginners are included in the resource list for this chapter at the end of the book. Experiment until you find a method that feels right to you.

Consider writing a short note in a diary after you meditate each morning. This confirms what you are reaching for as you meditate. Read the previous week's notes at the end of each week.

You Are Not Your Thoughts or Feelings Meditation Exercise

Find a quiet spot where you can sit for the next ten minutes. When you're comfortably settled, do the following:

1. Take a few slow, deep breaths.

2. Turn your attention to your thoughts. (If you tend to be an emotional person, you can do the same with your emotions.)

   Instead of getting caught up in your thoughts (or emotions) as you might usually do, watch them closely, the way an angler watches the tip of a rod or a tennis player watches a ball. If you find your attention wandering, come back to the task at hand.

   At first, your mind may seem like wall-to-wall thoughts or emotions, and you may have difficulty determining where one thought leaves off and the next one begins. You may also find that certain thoughts or emotions keep recurring like popular tunes—for example, repetitive worries or favorite images or fantasies. If you're especially attentive, you may begin to notice that each thought or emotion has its own constituent parts, including a beginning, a middle and an end.

3. At the end of the ten minutes, stop and reflect on your experience.

   Did you experience some "distance" from your thoughts or emotions? Or did you keep losing yourself in the thinking or feeling process?

   The point of this exercise is not to see how well you can track your thinking or feeling, but to give you the experience of being the observer of your thoughts.

Believe it or not, you're the thinker not the thoughts! As you begin to gain some perspective on your thoughts through the practice of meditation, you may find that they start losing the power they once had over you. You can have your thoughts, but they won't have you.[28]

Yoga

Taking a yoga class is my favorite way to get totally focused and clear my mind. I've gone to yoga class feeling distracted, excited or worried, and without fail, after an hour and a half of strenuous poses and paying attention to my breathing, I leave feeling calm, grounded and at peace.

Wayne Lehrer, yoga instructor at Inner Power Yoga in Calabasas, California, explains, "Yoga is an active form of meditation, but it's easier for our active, Western minds to focus on yoga than when we're sitting quietly trying to concentrate on a mantra or on the breath."

There are three aspects of this mental focus:

1. Focus on your inhale and exhale and use your mind to make them of equal length, duration and intensity.
2. Use your mind to focus on moving with grace and fluidity.
3. Press into your areas of physical tension and resistance, and use your mind to release and let that tension go.

This keeps you in the moment, which is the purpose of meditation.

---

[28] From *Meditation for Dummies*® by Stephen Bodian. ©1999 by Wiley Publishing, Inc. All rights reserved. Reproduced here by permission of the publisher.

CHAPTER EIGHT

The Path Is the Goal

"Man plans, God laughs"

— YIDDISH PROVERB

"Make them measurable and realistic! Make sure they'll get you to stretch, but don't make them out of reach! Did I mention you have to give yourself a deadline?!"

That drill sergeant was one of my business teachers. And for most of us, her goal-setting tips were better than the procrastination, wishful thinking or total avoidance of any planning process that we were stuck in when we got that advice. But there are big problems with that traditional method. When we pick measurable, realistic and specific objectives, we break down our overall mission that guides our work in order to focus on a few details. Without this meaningful context, these details can become chores that don't hold our interest. Or worse, focusing on one measurable detail of our work without seeing how it fits into the whole picture of our personal, family and career goals allows us to *lose our*

221

focus on our mission, which is what gives our careers and lives a sense of purpose.

Let's look at two common examples of measurable objectives. First, here's a typical list of goals for a business that sells a product:

1. Increase sales 25 percent this year.
2. Add two new products to our existing line.
3. Hire three salespeople by the second quarter of the year.

Here's a list for a salesperson:

1. Increase salary to next level by end of year.
2. Get on two high-profile project teams this year.
3. Increase sales of salespeople who report to me by 25 percent by end of third quarter.

Have you tried to write these kinds of goals? Did you write yours during a training seminar? Or maybe your company requires you to write this kind of list with your supervisor as part of your annual review. These are just deadly boring to me. They don't include any explanation of *why* you want to increase your income by 25 percent, or why you *care* enough about your product to sell more of them. And are you going to be selling something people need? Why will their lives be better if they buy these things from you? The questions that could connect your list to your deeper values never seem to come up in these goal-setting exercises.

If you've written one of these lists, did you stick to your goals even if more suitable ones emerged as you worked your plan? Or did you give up as soon as you got back to tackling day-to-day problems, forgetting about the quarterly or annual goals you had spelled out so carefully?

The Dangers of Most Goal-Setting Methods

Whether you set monetary goals, or goals to earn a particular job title or to get appointed to a specific project, there's a downside to most goal-setting methods.

Monetary Goals: Is the Price Too High?

Many consultants tell their clients to set monetary goals. They're measurable, have an obvious value and are assumed to reflect increasing success. But many of the burned-out clients I've seen, and others who've shared their stories via e-mail and over the phone, suffer from driving themselves to earn a dollar amount that doesn't have anything to do with their quality of life. Once you have enough money to live a safe, healthy and simple life, that's the end of money *substantially* contributing to your quality of life. Not because more money *couldn't* contribute in some way to making your life more meaningful. Having money is very handy, and if you have an emergency fund and are saving for retirement, it can reduce your stress level quite a bit. But focusing on material wealth as your main motivator is one of the best ways to become more *upwardly* mobile and less *inwardly* mobile. It's an external goal and doesn't specifically lead to finding meaning in your life.

"Years ago I made a decision to take a job simply because it would pay more than the other offer I was considering," says Craig Pisano, MBA, future entrepreneur. "I was pursuing two jobs, both very different from each other. I was living at home at the time, and my parents' advice was simple. Take the job that paid more. I knew they loved me, and their advice seemed to make sense. So I followed it and started my new job. I quit six months later.

"Your happiness is not something our society cares about. As long as things look good from the outside, everything's fine. You may not be in a happy marriage, but if you own a house, have kids, have a spouse, then you have the American dream. You may hate your job, but if you make a lot of money everyone will envy you. *I learned the hard way that to be truly happy I had to listen to myself, not to what society dictates.*"

Choosing a job based on a dollar amount seems like an easy way to make a hard decision. You can compare offers, you can compare yourself to what others earn and you can compare what you're making now to what you made last year. *But that's all it is—a primitive measuring stick.* Your salary doesn't tell you much about the quality of life you'll have once you earn enough to pay your bills. To get information about that, you have to dig a lot deeper. And you need to know what your values and priorities are. Don't avoid thinking about how much money you'll earn when choosing a job. Just see the dollar amount for what it is. It's the answer to a *small* question. Make sure you don't neglect the *big* questions that profoundly impact your quality of life just to get the answer to a very limited question.

External Goals: Can You Really Control the Important Ones?

Let's say you agree that setting a dollar amount as your goal may sabotage your ability to spend your time on what matters most. But you still think you should set an external goal—something measurable like a promotion or a particular job title. You may want to supervise your department, or chair a project with a bigger budget.

Or find another position based on external factors like how your job duties appear to others, and whether you'll inspire at least a little career envy when you hand out your business card.

Although conventional wisdom would say that you're bright and ambitious, there are several problems with this method of choosing your next position. First of all, most people can't get past the idea that they have to be moving along on a straight upward path. They see position and salary as indicators of success, and if these are moving up, they're going in the right direction. If they go down, they're failing. This is the most superficial way to judge their career and their level of success, but most people use this method of deciding what to do next in their careers long after it's failed to point them toward a meaningful job they can feel good about.

One danger of targeting a particular position is that you'll end up planning for the next rung on the ladder based almost completely on what you're currently doing, even if you don't enjoy your job. And you probably won't plan to get into a position that pays you less or isn't a move up the food chain, even if that would be a job which would be a great match for you. That territory would be off your map.

Planning for a specific job is more about reducing our anxiety about the unknown aspects of our future than it is about making smart career choices.

Second, when we're trying to plan a future career, we have a limited vantage point of what the best opportunity will be. If we try to plan something as specific as a particular job ahead of time, we ignore the fact that opportunities will come up that we *couldn't have anticipated*. Some of them will be more meaningful and fulfilling than whatever is the next rung up the ladder from the job we have now. So when we think we can sit down with a pad of paper and plan our careers in detail, we're assuming that we can anticipate most future opportunities. Since this is impossible, I think it shows that this type of planning process is more about reducing our anxiety about the unknown aspects of our future than it is about making smart career choices.

Trail Marker: *If you feel anxious because you don't know what your next career step will be, acknowledge the feeling, but don't take action simply to make the anxiety go away. Instead, exercise, meditate or take a hot bath. Anxiety tells us, "Do something!" But it's better to wait until the anxiety passes, and act based on a deeper part of ourselves.*

The Dangers of Not Planning: Ignorance Can Be Agony

"If I'd known what my home life was going to be like I wouldn't have started the school," says Debi Corso, Founder of Seven Peaks Elementary School in Bend, Oregon. "I pretty much tried not to think ahead to what my day-to-day life would be like, because I was afraid I wouldn't have gone ahead with the school if I planned it out ahead of time. But because I didn't plan ahead, my health got sacrificed, my mood, being with my kids, having fun. There was definitely a huge price to pay."

Debi did a lot of things right. Her goal was meaningful to her and was designed to improve her children's quality of life. Her husband was supportive and was an actively involved parent. But she didn't accurately predict how much her life, and the lives of her children and husband, would be disrupted while she worked to achieve this goal.

I've heard countless other entrepreneurs say that if they'd known what starting their own business would actually be like, they would never have done it. But this comment is usually made looking back in amazement at how challenging the process was. And it's usually said with a feeling of satisfaction, glad that they didn't know the rough road that was ahead of them at the beginning, and glad that they met most of the challenges. But if you have young children at home, or have top priorities other than working, you may not feel very good looking back at what you've sacrificed, and what you've volunteered your children to sacrifice.

Debi underestimated both how much time she would spend on starting up a new school, and how much time she'd spend thinking about it when she wasn't physically working on it.

I spent a lot of time on things that didn't pan out, but were still necessary, like searching for a site for the school and other time-consuming activities. But I did a lot of things that weren't a smart use of my time. Like time spent thinking about business while I was with my family. My kids just like to know I'm physically there sometimes. But a lot of the time I wasn't physically there, and when I was, I often wasn't mentally there for them. They stopped coming to me with questions or demands. I felt really guilty. John, my husband, would fill in and take over with the kids . . . a lot like a single parent.

I completely underestimated how intense the experience of starting a business would be. I wasn't objective since I was so mentally involved in the project. It was another baby.

For a year and a half while I started up the business, my family's quality of life stunk. It put a tremendous strain on our marriage. And it was even harder on the kids, like I was saying. And I really neglected myself and the things I enjoy. I completely underestimated how intense the experience of starting a business would be. I wasn't objective since I was so mentally involved in the project. It was another baby.

The answer isn't simply to avoid monetary and external goals. Like Debi, you may have a goal based on your values and priorities. But when you select a career goal without examining the toll it will take on your family and personal life, you can easily sacrifice your quality of life. If you use the Synergy Planning tools in this book, you can create a workable plan that keeps your priorities intact.

You might be wondering, if planning the details of my career actually *gets in the way* of following the natural flow of my career path, what kind of planning *should* I do?

The Inwardly Mobile Goal-Setting Method: The Path Is the Goal

I call my method of planning, "The Path is the Goal" because I'm not suggesting that you choose an ending point and find the fastest way to get there. Instead, I want you to choose a starting point and identify guideposts along the way that will let you know whether you're on the right path. Or if you've strayed from it before you've gone too far.

This accomplishes several things:

• You're leaving lots of room for opportunities to come up that you *couldn't have* planned for when you started out.

- You're increasing the chances that opportunities that come your way will allow you to develop and express your true self.
- You'll have some warning signs if you're straying from your values and priorities.

It's a trade-off. You give up trying to guess the particular spot where you'll end up, and you gain something much more important. If you can cope with the anxiety of not knowing precisely where you're going, you can point yourself toward a career path that will present you with choices that you'll be satisfied with no matter which *particular* opportunity you choose. In other words, you know that wherever you end up, you'll be doing something that you care about and that allows you to spend your life on what's meaningful and satisfying to you.

Fitting in the Big Rocks

Steven Covey shares the following story in his book *First Things First*.

> One of our associates shared this experience:
> I attended a seminar once where the instructor was lecturing on time. At one point, he said, 'Okay, it's time for a quiz.' He reached under the table and pulled out a wide-mouth gallon jar. He set it on the table next to a platter with some fist-sized rocks on it. 'How many of these rocks do you think we can get in the jar?' he asked.
> After we made our guess, he said, 'Okay. Let's find out.' He set one rock in the jar . . . then another . . . then another. I don't remember how many he got in, but he got the jar full. Then he asked, 'Is that jar full?'
> Everybody looked at the rocks and said, 'Yes.'

Then he said, 'Ahhh.' He reached under the table and pulled out a bucket of gravel. Then he dumped some gravel in and shook the jar and the gravel went in all the little spaces left by the big rocks. Then he grinned and said once more, 'Is the jar full?'

By this time we were on to him. 'Probably not,' we said.

'Good!' he replied. And he reached under the table and brought out a bucket of sand. He started dumping the sand in and it went in all the little spaces left by the rocks and the gravel. Once more he looked at us and said, 'Is the jar full?'

'No!' we all roared.

He said, 'Good!' and he grabbed a pitcher of water and began to pour it in. He got something like a quart of water in that jar. Then he said, 'Well, what's the point?'

Somebody said, 'Well there are gaps, and if you really work at it, you can always fit more into your life.'

'No,' he said, 'that's not the point. The point is this: If you hadn't put these big rocks in first, would you ever have gotten any of them in?'[29]

The big rocks are, of course, our priorities and values. I don't know if the speaker was able to convince this ambitious group of businesspeople of this, but leaving top priorities, important responsibilities and values out of the planning process is the worst problem of all with traditional business or career planning strategies. They leave the biggest issues off the map. They're expected to somehow fit in later, but of course, you feel like the most important parts of your life are just squeezed in, if they fit at all. What results

---

[29] Source: *First Things First.* Stephen R. Covey, A. Roger Merrill, Rebecca R. Merrill. Copyright 1994 Franklin Covey Co. Reprinted with permission. All rights reserved. Pp. 88–89.

is that there is the *least* room for what you feel is *most* important. This is a reliable recipe for stress, frustration and burnout. And it's the reason so many people feel that no matter how hard they work, they aren't getting anywhere. They're not spending most of their time on what they really care about.

It's one thing to say that we should fit in our values-based "big rocks" first. It's another to observe how we spend our time day-to-day. I like the analogy of a growing tree. The deep roots are our values and our purpose in life. We can't see them from above ground but they're the cause of all of our action. Our priorities are the branches. They're above ground and can be seen if you look closely, but they're hidden by hundreds or thousands of leaves. Those leaves are our actions. They are the easiest part of our values system to see. But they're only the *result*, not the *cause* of these deeply rooted values.

If you want to achieve success on *your terms*, your actions have to be based on your priorities, which are based on your values and your purpose in life or calling. Don't start by worrying about each leaf. Once you have healthy roots and branches, the leaves pretty much take care of themselves.

If you want to achieve success on *your terms*, your actions have to be based on your priorities, which are based on your values and your purpose in life or calling. Don't start by worrying about each leaf. Once you have healthy roots and branches, the leaves pretty much take care of themselves.

Start with Your Mission Statement

The foundation of Synergy Planning is your Mission Statement. It should help you point yourself toward a path that allows you to:

- Express your true self, which means that you'll automatically have a unique niche for your business or career.
- Grow as a person, not just accumulate possessions or climb someone else's ladder.
- Feel more and more comfortable in your own skin.

To Do: If you haven't yet worked on your Mission Statement, go back to that worksheet now (found in chapter 6.)

Your Unique Career Path Will Create Opportunities You Couldn't Have Thought of Ahead of Time

"I know I can't do this any more," says Deborah, a serious twenty-nine-year-old Human Resources director for a medium-size corporation. "I'm exhausted. I wish I knew what my calling is, but I don't have a clue. All I know is that I want to be a good mother to my son and a more available wife."

"Have you ever thought about what you might enjoy doing? Or have you ever met anyone and envied what they're doing?", I asked, not sure how I could help her access what seemed to be a deeply buried spark of passion.

Deborah paused a moment, as if she weren't sure if what she was about to say was too half-baked to share. She decided to give it a try. "I've always wanted to open my own place for families with little kids to get together for playdates and have birthday parties," Deborah said, lighting up for the first time. "My friends and the relatives that live nearby always ask me to help them put on parties for their kids, and I really enjoy it. I feel like a kid again when I see them having so much fun," she smiled, sitting up a little taller on the couch. "But is that a business idea?" She leaned back again, unsure how she could translate her enthusiasm into a business.

After seeing how Deborah had transformed from a bored and burned out manager to an enthusiastic would-be entrepreneur, I encouraged her to flesh out her idea between meetings. She was going to think through some of the details, and find out who else is doing something similar so that she could interview them about their experiences. (I use that method a lot. People who are passionate about what they do are almost always glad to share their experiences with someone else who has similar interests. And you can learn how to avoid common pitfalls, find out how established people in your chosen field actually spend their workdays and meet wonderful mentors this way.)

When Deborah came back a couple of weeks later, she seemed discouraged.

"It looks like I'd be competing with Gymboree and a couple of other private places that do playtimes and birthday parties. And the rents are so expensive in the area I had in mind, where there are a lot of stay-at-home moms who could use a break during the day."

Deborah had drafted her Mission Statement, so I turned to that before we went any further. "*I want to offer a safe, fun place for parents and kids to have special time together, and where parents can relax and play with their kids.*" It was a pretty good Mission Statement, but it was completely based on opening up this kind of facility.

I asked Deborah to write a more general Mission Statement that included her family and personal needs, and a big picture of what she wants to offer as a businessperson. Then we talked about different directions that she could take her business once she let go of the specific picture she had in mind.

Her new Mission Statement was a better starting point. "*I want to offer parents and kids a way to have special time together, and a way for parents to relax and play with their kids. And I want to have the time and energy to do the same with my family."* The main elements were there, and she had integrated her family. This opened up her possibilities much wider.

There were many directions that Deborah's path could take her. She might:

- Buy a franchise, like Gymboree or Mad Science, so that she doesn't have to build a small business from the ground up.
- Freelance as a party planner for families with young children, perhaps focusing her initial marketing efforts on word of mouth from those friends and relatives who were already sold on her skills, and on working parents who had more money than time to plan fun parties for their children and who didn't get much of a chance to relax and play with their kids and spouses.
- Write articles or a book about party planning for kids and conduct workshops teaching parents how to plan their own fun parties (or they could hire her, of course).

As Deborah plans out one of the many business ideas she's developing, she'll be meeting others who market to parents and she'll be speaking to prospective customers to find out what their needs are and what they're willing to pay for. And while she's in the process of planning her path, she'll be discovering other opportunities she hadn't thought about before she started fleshing out her business plan and networking. One of those opportunities might be even a better choice for her.

To Do: Now that you've created or reviewed and revised your

Mission Statement, take another look at your Family & Personal Goals and Guideposts worksheet (on page 167.) Then review your Career & Business Goals and Guideposts worksheet (on page 173.)

Do you need to clarify the goals listed on those worksheets? Do you see any common threads running through each list of goals that you can bring out and focus on? Do any of your goals or guideposts seem less essential upon review? Did you leave out something important? Revise these worksheets now. Start with the Family & Personal Goals and Guideposts. Then do your Career & Business Goals and Guideposts. Remember, big rocks first!

Putting It All Together

Now that you've reviewed and revised your previous worksheets, you're ready to put all of the pieces together. So far, you've been designing your guideposts and the first stretch of road for your path. Now you're going to put these in place and start taking your first steps along that path, which will lead you to opportunities you can't see from here. But they'll be in line with your mission, and they'll be deeper than the ones that are easily visible from the beginning since they're farther down your unique path.

I've included a client's worksheet as a sample. But use the blank worksheet (that follows the sample) to write your own plan.

E-mail from Julie

Subj: Update . . . great news!
From: julie@bigcompany.com

Hey Leslie!!

I have some great news. I have joined a firm here in NYC three days a week and am doing communications coaching—primarily oral, but I'm also doing some work around their written materials, which I love. I am getting all the female clients, so I'm continuing my work with women in organizations, which is important to me.

I fell into this when I was investigating career counseling, and it's a great fit for me. I use my extra two days a week to enjoy myself! I'm still doing some consulting work, and have a few private clients, whom I really enjoy. I'm active in my professional association, and all in all, life is good!

I'll be out in San Francisco in March, and was recently interviewed on the radio about E-networking, which was exciting.

Mark and Joe are fine. I hope all is well with you.

All the best,
Julie

Synergy Plan℠ Worksheet:
The Path Is the Goal *(Sample)*[30]

A. Mission Statement:

To help families learn to manage their finances so they can keep more of what they earn and spend more time doing what they value most in life.

B. Goals and Guideposts:

1. Personal Goals and Guideposts:

I want to take care of myself physically, mentally and spiritually. I want to make sure I have time to exercise, go to church and read.

2. Family Goals and Guideposts:

I want to be home when my children get home from school. I want to have more energy for my husband and children, and be more mentally present when I'm with them.

3. Career & Business Goals and Guideposts:

I want a flexible schedule, and I want to focus my coaching work on helping families interested in changing their financial habits so they can live by their values and teach their children to have a healthy relationship with money.

C. Ideas for my Career:

1. Money Coach

2. _____

---

[30] Filled out by Shirley Oya, Money Coach.

D. Starting Point of Career & Business Path:

Describe your role if an employee, or your business if you're planning a start-up. (Pick one idea per worksheet. Copy the worksheet to use if you want to sketch out more than one idea. Worksheets are also available on my Web site: *www.lesliegodwin.com*)

I'll use my accounting background and debt management skills to help families get (and stay out of) debt, and to plan for their future. I can meet them at their homes or offices. I'll need to structure my program and create worksheets and tipsheets, develop marketing materials, set my fees and create business cards.

E. Background Info:

What will this look like in two years? What will my role be?

1. Talk to:
   —*Friends, acquaintances, minister . . . get reactions about my idea*
   —*Possible referral sources; start networking with accountants, financial investment planners, personal and business coaches, and psychotherapists*

2. Think about:
   —*Who are my ideal clients; write a detailed profile*
   —*Pricing*
   —*What will help clients change their spending habits*
   —*Who else to network with*

3. Research:
   —*Statistics re. numbers of families in debt*

—Find out about: length of time carried debt, how and why got into debt, which bad habits make their debt worse, what they identify as the problem and what obstacles they perceive to getting and staying out of debt.

—What methods work to help people get out of debt and stay out of debt

F. Market Research:

Who will pay me? What will they pay? What are barriers to entry? How to get started? Who can help?

1. Talk to:
   —Possible referral sources
   —Check on Internet to see who else is doing this and what is their niche/angle

2. Who can help or mentor me:
   —Use a coach to help me quickly get business structured, answer questions
   —Network with other coaches to find out how they get clients, price their services
   —Therapist (Joanne) to go over workshop ideas and outline[31]
   —Is there a professional association of people in this field?

3. Possible points of entry:
   —Meet with minister to offer workshop at church for families in debt, families who want to live on less money so mom can stay home, and/or engaged or newlywed couples.

---

[31] This is a friend of Shirley's, not someone she sees for therapy. Joanne is willing to give Shirley pointers on her workshop outline.

G. What to Do:

1. Now:

—*Call minister*

—*Printer: get business cards to start networking (use a tagline, quote, or part of my Mission Statement on back of card)*

—*Find networking group*

2. Near Future:

—*Get letterhead, envelopes, note paper to match cards*

—*Draft several tip sheets covering common dilemmas and advice*

—*Gather e-mail addresses for future e-mailing of tips, announcements of workshops, etc. (Consider doing an e-mail newsletter.)*

3. After That:

—*Web site or brochure*

—*Workshops at my church, other churches, local adult ed.—take class on public speaking*

—*Press releases, especially before and after Christmas/Chanukah: address holiday spending and New Year's resolutions to get out of debt*

Synergy Plan℠ Worksheet: The Path Is the Goal *(Blank)*

A. Mission Statement:

B. Goals and Guideposts:
   1. Personal Goals and Guideposts:
   2. Family Goals and Guideposts:
   3. Career/Business Goals and Guideposts:

C. Ideas for my Career:
   1. _____
   2. _____

D. Starting Point of Career & Business Path:
Describe your role if an employee, or your business if you're planning a start-up. (Pick one idea per worksheet. Copy the worksheet to use if you want to sketch out more than one idea. Worksheets are also available on my Web site: *www.lesliegodwin.com*)

E. Background Info:
What will this look like in two years? What will my role be?
   1. Talk to: _____

   _____

   2. Think about: _____

   _____

   3. Research: _____

   _____

F. Market Research:

What is needed? Who will pay me? What will they pay? Barriers to entry? How to get started? Who can help?

1. Talk to: _____

_____

2. Who can help or mentor me: _____

_____

3. Possible points of entry: _____

_____

G. What to Do:

1. Now: _____

_____

2. Near Future: _____

_____

3. After That: _____

_____

How Supportive Is Your Support System?

I started using the next worksheet with my coaching clients because each one had at least one person in their life that they anticipated would undermine their efforts to follow their new path.

It's incredibly frustrating to work hard to uncover hidden dreams and aspirations, then map out a plan to follow, only to be discouraged as you take the first anxious but excited steps on that path.

We're very vulnerable when we start out into unfamiliar territory. And especially so because this new path represents being more real and true to ourselves. So any criticism or sarcastic remark feels like more of a personal attack than if the reaction were related to something less representative of who we really are.

Have you ever written a poem or journal entry that was very personal? Did you show it to anyone? If you did, it wasn't to have them correct your grammar. You probably shared it with a trusted friend as a way to share a bit of yourself with them.

I urge you to respect how vulnerable you might feel when you act on a plan that's based on who you are and what you care about most. The following worksheet can help you both avoid sharing it too soon with anyone who might sabotage your efforts, and to find the inspiration and support from those who share your passionate interest. You'll also identify people who support you becoming who you're meant to be.

Saboteurs

*The reasonable man adapts himself
to the world; the unreasonable one persists in
trying to adapt the world to himself.
Therefore, all progress depends
on the unreasonable man.*

—George Bernard Shaw

I want to clarify what I mean when I say that there are people who would sabotage your efforts. I don't mean that you're surrounded by troublesome friends and acquaintances who wish for you to fail. That's pretty rare. But most of us have friends and family who want us to do something safe, or that makes sense to them, because they care about us.

And the more sensitive we are, the easier it is to knock us off balance with a comment, a look or even *not* saying something we'd like to hear.

"I was frustrated," tells Robin, a forty-three-year-old personal-success coach. "I was receiving very little support from people around me, including my husband, because it appeared that I was 'throwing away' my years in communications. I became convinced that I was just going through a phase, and that there must be something wrong with me to want to walk away from a solid career based on the degree I had earned. No one from my past could picture me as a speaker or the catalyst I felt like, except a couple of people who knew it all along. And they made no secret of that."

Maybe it's fitting that the struggle to find your path is an isolated experience in many ways. For one thing, the process is something that only you can do. Even if you work with a coach or a therapist, you alone have to go through what poets, philosophers and Van Morrison refer to as the "dark night of the soul." It's a one-person job. The other part of the process is that as you grow, you grow out of certain relationships. And those who do grow with you will change in the process.

It's both a blessing and a curse to be rejected by those you have relied on in some way. If the curse is feeling isolated just when you're vulnerable and confused, then the blessing is that you're forced to think for yourself. And you're spared some really awful advice.

I'll bet that the people in Robin's life who felt compelled to warn her that she is "throwing away" a career she worked hard to build felt that they were being helpful. But what kind of advice is that? To tell someone who is unhappy with their career to stick with it when they've identified something they might really enjoy seems cruel. These people, like many of your peers and relatives, are probably not sadists or even mostly motivated by envy (although that is usually a factor to *some* degree). They're anxious for you about the unknown path you are entering upon as you leave the safety of the familiar, but confining, world you've created for yourself.

Once you begin to tap into your true self and feel grounded, you won't need as much approval from others, especially those who don't understand or value what you're trying to do.

You can be proactive in this period of your personal growth by:

1. Looking inward for guidance rather than outside yourself.
2. Reducing your need to consult others who don't have real wisdom to offer.

3. Continuing to deepen your understanding of your inner world, and resist the temptations that bring you back up to the surface of life.

The prospect of losing external support, and dealing with the changes in some of your relationships, can be very intimidating to some people. For those of us who are either fairly introverted, or have difficult relationships to begin with, this is less challenging. We're motivated to change the status quo and the changes can make our lives more pleasurable and easier, so there's less ambivalence. But if you're outgoing, or don't like to rock the boat in relationships, even if they aren't rewarding, this can be a major roadblock to your progress.

The next worksheet, Support Systems, can help you clarify who supports your efforts to uncover your calling and pursue a more meaningful life and who is likely to discourage you (even if they mean well).

Who do you have in your life who helps you stay true to yourself? Who do you look up to in your chosen field? Who might not know much about your field, but believes in you as a person and encourages you to find and follow your calling?

Make a note of these "angels" in your life in the worksheet on the next page. You'll meet others once you get started on your path and you can add them later.

> *The first, easiest and most obvious*
> *assistance toward an individual's private*
> *efforts is the simple association with*
> *others making the same attempt.*
>
> —RAMANA MAHARSHI
> FAMOUS TWENTIETH-CENTURY INDIAN MYSTIC

Synergy Plan℠ Worksheet:
Support Systems

1. What kind of support system do you think will help you find and stay on your path?

(Example: an informal group of friends and colleagues you call as needed, an advisory board of mentors you meet with quarterly, a networking group where everyone helps each other and meets frequently, or?)

_____

_____

_____

_____

2. Who can you count on to help and encourage you, and what kind of support can you ask them for?

Name	Relationship	Kind of Support
example: Jane	*Informal mentor*	*Can introduce me to experts in my field who I can learn from*
example: Samantha	*Generally supportive of my inner development*	*Can help me remember why I'm doing this when I have a bad day.*

3. Who might *not* be very supportive?

(List people you may need to keep out of the loop until you're more sure about your path.)

_____

_____

_____

_____

4. Is there anyone who may not be supportive who is important to your success?
(your family, boss or spouse, for example)

_____

_____

_____

_____

5. How can you help them understand the importance of following your path? How can you gain some support from them? If that is not likely right now, how can you ensure they don't discourage or distract you from your path and related goals?

_____

_____

_____

_____

6. Who else would you like to add to your support system? How will you approach them and when will you take that action?

Name and/or Position	How to Approach	When Will You Take Action
_____	_____	_____
_____	_____	_____
_____	_____	_____
_____	_____	_____
_____	_____	_____
_____	_____	_____

Mentoring Can Help You Stay on Track

Once you've begun to make the internal shift to following your path and ignoring your inner critic, and you're working on developing a support system that encourages you to follow your calling and express your true self, a mentoring relationship—both being mentored and mentoring others—can help you stay on track. It's important to choose advisers based on their values and their ability to lead their lives in a way you admire. When you have an ongoing relationship with such a mentor, you're furthering your commitment to growing as a person. You also further that commitment when you give back to others by mentoring them. Few relationships offer so much to both parties.

Don't be intimidated by the idea of a formal mentor relationship. You can start out with an informal relationship. (Although many professional organizations have excellent structured mentor programs.) Get to know someone who has the potential to mentor you. Then take them to lunch or meet them at their office. Follow up on the advice they give you and see if they seem to be getting something out of the relationship, too.

The same goes for establishing a mentor relationship with a mentee. Be available, offer to help and return calls when someone does want your advice. Then see how the relationship develops.

I'll describe both being mentored and mentoring others, and I'll include the experiences of a few people who have done one or the other.

Being Mentored

What exactly is a mentor? A mentor is someone who has some or all of the following qualities:

- The ability to see your situation as an outside observer, and who won't get overwhelmed by what overwhelms you
- Wisdom, not just intelligence and experience
- The desire to be of service
- The ability to tell you what you need to hear, not what you want to hear
- May have experience or contacts in your field

Most important, they live based on their values and have values you respect.

A mentor may be a:

- Listener
- Confidant
- Cheerleader
- Coach
- Tutor

A mentor is not a:

- Savior
- Parent
- Therapist
- ATM machine or loan officer
- Legal counselor
- Usually not a friend (in order to stay objective and tell you the truth)

Example: Being Mentored

"I had worked in international customer service for a manufacturer my mentor's company distributed," tells Amanda. "Joel phoned me one day and offered me a sales position with his company's branch office in Miami, Florida. The offer was unexpected, and my background didn't include sales experience. I never misrepresented myself, but Joel still felt certain I'd be great at the position. At twenty-three, it was pretty heady stuff to be noticed and inspire the confidence of someone already so successful. I told him I'd take the position on one condition, that I could come to him at any time I thought I needed guidance. He agreed, and I took the job.

"Joel was true to his word. During the five-plus years I worked for his company, he never let me down, even when supporting me gave him exposure he didn't need at a higher level. The best advice he ever gave me? 'Don't go out and try to sell at all costs. No sales quota is ever worth your integrity. Go out and make friends. People turn to their friends because they genuinely care. Be a friend. People will buy from you, and you'll never have to worry about meeting a quota.'"

—*Amanda, sales manager*

Example: Being Mentored

Michelle Hazlewood, personal trainer and author, told me about her mentor. She was Michelle's manager at a health club. "The main thing that impressed me about her was her unselfish honesty. She told me that while I was the best employee on her staff, she felt she needed to tell me that I could do much better on my own. Then she helped me find the tools to actually pull it off."

—*Michelle Hazlewood, owner of Universal Wellness and author of the* Personal Success Guide for the 21st Century

Being a Mentor

What can you expect to get from being a mentor?

- An opportunity to offer your wisdom and guidance to someone who will appreciate your talents and skills
- An opportunity to learn something new about yourself and your field
- An opportunity to serve others in a meaningful way
- An opportunity to make a difference in someone's career and possibly their life
- An opportunity to give back as a way of giving thanks to those people who have formally or informally mentored you
- Your mentee's sincere thanks and appreciation for all of your efforts

Example: Being a Mentor

Laurie Dea Owyang, president of the human resources consulting firm Humanasaurus, has been mentoring people for many years. She mentors others in her professional life and in her volunteer activities (including the YWCA, Professionals in Human Resources Association and local schools) "because others have helped me, and continue to help me, along the way. It feels good to pass on wisdom and life experience to others knowing it will help them expedite their goals. I feel strongly that mentees should just ask, because people are generally willing to help others. Never be too shy to approach someone else who is more experienced because they are usually happy to help."

—*Laurie Dea Owyang, president,*
Humanasaurus, Human Resources Consultants

Example: Being a Mentor

Mariaemma Willis told me that her mentor relationship with a homeschooling client has been extremely rewarding to her. She says that this mentee's "life has dramatically changed because I encouraged and coached her to do something she has wanted to do all her life, but that everyone else said would never work. It's such a great feeling to know I had a part in helping her in this way."

—*Mariaemma Willis, Learning-Success™ coach*
and coauthor of Discover Your Child's Learning Style

PART FOUR

REACH HIGHER

CHAPTER NINE

Beyond Balance
to Meaning

"I had a lot of great habits," explains Reverend Sandra Yarlott, Director of Spiritual Care at UCLA Medical Center, (whom I quoted in chapter 5.)

Reverend Yarlott continues, "Exercise, eating healthy, balancing spiritual practice and work and friendships . . . but they were habits. They weren't internalized. It wasn't until I stopped in my tracks and entered the silence that the habits shifted to ways of being. It was sitting in the silence that made the transformation possible. I found a deeper place inside myself that I'd never been to before. . . .

"I think balance is a step in the direction that's going to bring us to more meaning, but it's not sufficient. We do need a balance between meaningful work, relationships and time with the self. But the piece we neglect the most is cultivating your spiritual self. You have to cultivate the connection with your spiritual self to have meaning. For some, it's being alone in nature. For others, it's journal writing. For others, it's a meditation practice. You can feed the ego's wants and needs, but that's never going to lead to an expanded sense of being or meaning."

What we're after isn't just balance; it's meaning. So you can't simply draw a circle on a piece of paper and decide how big a slice you want each part of your life to be. There's an integrity to the whole that happens when you're in tune with your true self. You feel like you're in the right place at the right time. You don't feel like you're forcing anything to work. It's the difference between paddling frantically upstream and riding the current going downstream.

It's important to realize that a career can't provide certain essential elements of a full and rewarding life. The purpose of Synergy Planning is to aim beyond merely living a balanced life and to aspire for a meaningful, passionate life.

Not an Intellectual Exercise: We Need to Experience an Internal Shift

I hope you found the descriptions of the types of burnout, and my advice for changing your relationship to work and to yourself, helpful. But even if you have put your heart and soul into the worksheets and exercises in this book, until a major internal shift occurs at a deep level, your enthusiasm will fade, this book and its worksheets will gather dust, and you'll slowly go back to orbiting the strong gravitational forces of your ego, its desires, and your daily chores and activities. You'll feel the pull of your soul or true self, too, but without the purposeful emphasis on that higher part of you, it's natural to give in to gravity and sink down to the lower parts.

When an addict or codependent decides to try a twelve-step program (like Alcoholics Anonymous), they're told to go to ninety meetings in ninety days. That's because what AA has to offer is not an intellectual exercise. Yes, you do have to learn the content. But it's more important to practice reacting differently to stressors until you start to expand your consciousness. Then you'll have other, better options than the reflexive ones that come naturally, but that cause pain and keep you stuck.

The most rewarding part of my work as both a coach and as a psychotherapist might be when I see a client go from reacting to a hurtful situation, to trying out a new response. It's a magical moment.

Janice, a thirty-two-year-old client, recently had one of those moments. She came in to my office and started explaining what had happened as soon as she sat down. She had occasionally complained that her husband, Joe, would leave his laundry on the floor instead of putting it in the hamper. On a good day, she didn't care too much. But when she was having a tough day, this really got on her nerves and made her feel taken for granted.

"I was having one of those days," Janice said, anxious to tell me about her experience. "I was feeling unloved, unhappy and hormonal. I walked by the bedroom and saw Joe's shorts, t-shirt and underwear lying on the floor. He must have just dumped his gym bag onto the bedroom floor. I lost it. First I felt angry. But pretty soon I sat down on the bed and started to cry." Janice took a Kleenex out of the box on the side table at the end of the couch and held onto it while her eyes filled with tears, remembering how flooded with emotion she'd felt a few days earlier.

"I cried for a few minutes. It surprised me. I've been irritated at Joe's laundry on the floor, but I never felt *sad* about it. It didn't make sense. I guess my surprise at all that crying made me wonder where it came from. I tried to let my mind go blank to see what would come up. The thought popped into my head that Joe loves me and he doesn't throw his laundry on the floor because he thinks of me as his maid. He does it when he's just gotten back from working out and the kids are following him, wanting to play. If I leave his stuff there a day or two, he picks it up and puts it in the hamper.

"As soon as I realized this, I felt a huge relief—this whole anger about his dirty laundry that irritated me once or twice a week was gone. Yesterday, Joe left his towel on the floor. When I went over to put it in the hamper I realized that I'd be lying to myself if I got all upset and told myself that he didn't respect me or treated me like a maid. It was like that part of me was an immature teenager and the calmer and more detached part was me the adult."

When we shift from reacting emotionally and feeling out of control of our emotions and behavior, to taking a step back into the "witness" position, we're not just using our minds to think differently or learning a new tool to use when we're stressed. We're growing and developing a new part of ourselves. A part that is connected to something higher that isn't controlled by our thoughts or feelings. But once we open ourselves up to a higher energy, our thoughts *can* help us to *stay* on that higher plane when lower impulses try to get us to react.

There's No Finish Line for This Work

I've been encouraged along the way, both in my personal development and in writing this book, by others who have also found their unique path by nurturing their true self or soul and looking inward for meaning and truth about life and work.

Some of the encouragement came from books I read along the way. Some of these were spiritual and religious books. I'll include just a couple of them in the resources at the end of this chapter, because choosing which spiritual or religious books to read is very personal. I found that reading "how-to" books strictly for information wasn't nearly as meaningful as reading books that touched my soul and made me feel uplifted and as though I understood something deeper than if I'd just used my intellect. The best ones put me in a higher frame of mind, for lack of a better term. A frame of mind that was conducive to inner reflection and contemplation of something higher. They helped me to leave behind what now seem like petty preferences and lower impulses and fears.

I also spoke to quite a few people, both men and women, who had struggled with burnout, caring about what others thought of their career and family life, and battling their inner critic. These people were now living their lives according to what they cared about most, and looking inward and upward for answers. I'll include some of my interviews with them in the next section, Interviews with the Inwardly Mobile.

There's no finish line for this work. You just keep doing the best you can, and some days you can tune in to your intuition and calling more easily than other days. But if you have faith in the process and if you build up some momentum by making this inner work a practice, as opposed to hoping for some kind of sudden change that will make everything right from then on, you'll have more calm, grounded days than frantic, hectic, self-doubting days.

I'd very much like to hear from you. My contact information is at the end of the book on the page titled, "About the Author." Please let me know where you are along your journey, and any comments, questions or constructive criticism you have about this book. Thank you.

This is a book about inner reflection and finding your true self.

For those of you who are not comfortable with the terms "God" or "the Divine," you can read this book as a guide to living according to your true self and searching for the Truth and not just what feels good at the moment. And for those of you who are spiritual or religious, please expand on my comments based on your specific beliefs and faith.

> *Inner awakening seems to be met initially by outer deprivation . . . . Although you will not lose everything, you will lose everything that is false. . . . If there is anything that is fundamentally tragic in the human condition, it is this: life in illusion is not worth living, yet the road to illumination can be so painful.*
>
> *If this were all, the story would be a gloomy one indeed. Some have gone this far and no further: they are the nihilists and cynics of our era and of all eras. Staring into the emptiness of conventional reality, they have stopped there. But they have seen only a partial truth. They do not recognize that there is something beyond that will more than make up for these losses. It is the only thing in the world worth having, the "pearl of great price," for which a man sells all he has. It is yourself. It is the dawning of the true "I," the recognition that that in you which sees, which peers out at the world through the telescope that is your soul and body, is deathless and impervious to pain. All the great religious teachings point to this truth.*
>
> *To the extent that you possess this realization, you know you need nothing else. At first it will come and go, sometimes manifesting brightly and clearly, sometimes obscured by worries and cares. But if you persist, eventually you will begin to notice and trust in it more. Out of this feeling will arise a subtle but imperturbable joy.*

Even so, the way is not one of ceaseless sacrifice. Around the "I" a fresher, more vital world begins to constellate—new relationships, new forms of work, that are more in harmony with one's inner nature. This new life may well have nothing to do with success as usually understood—but it is likely to prove far more satisfying.[32]

[32] Richard Smoley. *Inner Christianity: A Guide to the Esoteric Tradition*. Boston: Shambhala Publications, Inc., 2002. pp. 242–243.

Interviews with the Inwardly Mobile

"You can hear your gut if you
turn down the noise."

—Margot Lester, Owner
The Word Factory, Writer and Consultant

Q: *Was there a moment when you realized you weren't on the right path, and that you needed to get on the right path for you regardless of the short-term consequences?*

A: My best friend was killed in a car accident in March of 1997. I was completely floored and took a month off to figure out what was really important. I was thirty-five. At his funeral, his brother said that the best way to keep his spirit alive was to take what you liked best about Gibson, and bring it to bear on your own lives. I really latched onto that. What I loved most about Gibson was that no matter when you saw him, or for how long, he was engaged with you and made you feel like he had waited all day to see you.

I realized at that point that I was living my life too fast, I wasn't available and accessible to people. You could always get me on the phone, but I wasn't really there. It was a defining moment. It was the best present Gibson ever gave me. I said to myself, I don't know what I'm going to do, but I'm going to live my life so that I make the people I care about a priority.

I lost my best friend, and got out of the printing business. Those two events created this clarity for me. What I really loved most besides people in my life was not public relations, even though I'm really good at it. But I wanted to write. And be engaged in my community, doing community journalism and having a flexible schedule. This is what I should be doing.

I had three amazing mentors. To a person, they said that I'm making the right decision. "You're a writer. Go with what you want to do." Having that external validation for something that my heart told me to do anyway made me feel bulletproof. They're not "yes men" and I always do what they say.

I left home, Chapel Hill, North Carolina, for the first time and came out to Los Angeles. I only knew two people and had no job prospects.

Q: *What were some of your challenges once you decided to live an authentic life?*

A: If you've had a certain level of success in something, it's hard to step away from that ride even if you're not crazy about it. Partly because of what other people will think, and also because you're stepping away from what has given you self-esteem. I was really lucky that I had a great support network. "The Gods will always look after you, but you have to put yourself in the path of the Gods" (Merlin in King Arthur's court said that).

Q: *What do you recommend to others?*

A: Phil Jackson wrote in *Sacred Hoops* that finding his own way included learning to turn down the noise of life so you can hear the natural rhythm. You can hear your gut if you turn down the noise. That's where you get the strength, conviction and the courage to make the change.

I wrote a play at six years old. My parents really encouraged me to write and it never became a chore. I got to keep that initial innocent love of writing, and was able to turn it into a career.

Favorite Books: *The Soul's Code: In Search of Character and Calling* by James Hillman: great exploration of the value of finding and following your calling, complete with examples from real life.

Getting to Where You Are: The Life of Meditation by Steven Harrison: a book of prose and tips on living in the moment and valuing what you have and are.

Favorite Web site: *www.google.com*

Favorite CD/Album: Frank Sinatra, *The Capitol Years*

Favorite Quote: "Just make it a little more artful."

—Stanley Tucci

"I went from 'doing the right thing'
to jumping into the 'void' and deciding to
pursue what was more meaningful to me, even
though I didn't know what that was yet."

—DAVID ALLEN, AUTHOR AND
OWNER OF THE DAVID ALLEN COMPANY

Q: *Was there a moment when you realized that you weren't on the right path, and that you needed to get on the right path regardless of the short-term consequences?*

A: I made a dramatic choice when I was in graduate school, when one day (at age twenty-three) I realized that I wasn't doing what I really wanted to be doing. I didn't know what that was, but I knew it wasn't being in graduate school. I went from "doing the right thing" to jumping into the "void" and deciding to pursue what was more meaningful to me, even though I didn't know what that was yet. So I did all kinds of pay-the-rent jobs while I went on a major inner self-exploration journey. That lasted at least twelve years, until in the early 1980s, when I finally began to get my feet on the ground with the kind of work that was both externally stimulating and internally aligned.

Q: *What do you feel is the purpose of your life?*

A: To know myself and God, and align my expression in the best possible way to reflect that.

Q: *What difficulties (if any) are there in living a more authentic life without retreating from the world entirely?*

A: Initially it was very painful to embark on this journey. I had lots of expectations about other people understanding and supporting me that weren't met by reality. A lot of the work on growing myself, however, involved becoming aware of what was mine, what was authentic and building relationships based much more on those truths.

Q: *What are your priorities and how do they affect your life now?*

A: To take care of the most important aspects of my life expression (health, spiritual awareness, significant relationships, personal resource management), do as much good work as I can and return to my loving expression no matter what.

Favorite book: *Tiger's Fang by Paul Twitchell*
Favorite Web site: *www.wsj.com (Wall Street Journal)*
Favorite CD: Diana Krall, *The Look of Love*
Favorite Quote: "We see by something which illumines us, something which we do not see." —Antonio Porchia

*"Something was breaking free inside of me
after being responsible for so much."*

—Diana Moore
Realtor

Q: *How did you change jobs from one that burned you out, to a less stressful career?*

A: I became disenchanted with mortgage banking, which I had gotten into to take care of my son after my divorce. At one point, I was executive vice president of operations for an international mortgage banking company, and was supervising 217 people. It was very stressful; I felt too responsible. Then, even though my division was making money and quality control was fine, headquarters in Canada decided to close it anyway. I spent three months closing down a business that I had spent thirteen years building up.

That year we had the big Northridge earthquake, my son started to have health problems and moved back in with me, and I wanted to do something simpler and not supervise so many people. But I didn't want to start over from scratch.

My job was no longer fun. I almost never interacted with people. Something was breaking free inside of me after being responsible for so much.

So I sent out thirteen resumes, and got two offers. I took another mortgage banking position for the short term, but one closer to my family, and my horse.

Q: *How did you start your own business as a real estate agent?*

A: It was after this last position as vice president of operations for Pacific Central Mortgage in Westlake, California, that I decided to begin my own business. I took some money from a 401k and gamely started out. The first year and a half was very scary, as I had had a position with a steady income plus bonus for so many years. I decided not to underwrite or process on the side for extra money since it required me to promise specific hours to companies and I needed to be fluid to serve my clients in real estate. I sat other peoples listings, did anything but door knocking and cold calling to try to create a clientele. My first break was being approved for Amgen's relocation agency. They didn't want salesmen, they wanted professionals to represent and care about their incoming employees.

Q: *You're a real estate agent now. Real estate can be a very stressful business, and not one known for ethical, caring agents. How do you make that work for you and not compromise your values and ethics?*

A: I don't consider myself a salesperson, first of all. I either market a property or represent my client. I'm not just trying to make a sale. Sales means to me that I'm trying to get someone to buy something they may not need or want.

I'm good at teaching, and I keep my clients ahead of the game. They never have to wonder what's going to happen next.

My clients are very loyal to me because I treat them with respect and always do what's in their best interest. This year I'll make more than I did in the mortgage banking position I got burned out on. I think I'm proof that you can make a good living by being a good person.

Q: *What would you say to yourself if you could meet the person you were at twenty-three when you were first searching for work about how to approach your career?*

A: Realize that time passes quickly. Rather than making the best of situations at hand, take the time to think about what you'd like to do best to earn a living. Don't ignore important parts of your life to strive for excellence in just a few areas. And listen to that old friend who told you to save 10 percent of your next raise.

I need to expand what I feel I'm capable of doing, while I continue to focus on what I care about. I suppose I should take a little of my advice since some parts of me are still twenty-three. I also hope to meet my mate . . . better late than never.

Favorite Books: *Pride and Prejudice* by Jane Austen, and *Kon-Tiki* by Thor Heyerdahl

Favorite Web sites: *www.ladygouldianfinch.com*. I keep fancy finches and this site has more information and is more beautiful than others I have found.

www.saddletude.com: A great place for sports information in many different equine disciplines.

Favorite CD/Album: Govi, *Guitar Odyssey* or any Mozart directed by Mariner. I also love early R&B.

Favorite Quote: "There are only two ways to live your life. One is as though nothing is a miracle. The other is as if everything is a miracle." —Albert Einstein

*"Being an artist is hard enough
without trying to fit into someone else's idea
of what being successful means."*

—Robert Laper
Artist, antique dealer, art and antique restoration

Q: How did you find your unique path?

A: Growing up I saw my father as his own boss and the freedom he had to do as he wished, when he wished. My grandmother was an artist and also had control over her schedule. I'm following in both of their footsteps.

I think it's the restless artist, little kid in me that constantly rebels against the 9 to 5 mentality. Funny thing is, I work from 7:00 A.M. to midnight some days! But that's my choice.

Q: What do you feel the purpose of your life is?

A: Next year, I'll be fifty. I still don't know what I want to be when I grow up. What I do know is that life shouldn't be just about surviving day-to-day, although that's what most of us, including myself at times, seem to be doing. I'm an artist. I also collect and sell antiques. I am constantly running across old photos with nothing written on the back to tell anything about who that person was. Nothing is known and nobody cares! I felt like that was my life . . . nothing will be known and other than my children, no one will really care. I decided that the only way to make my life really matter is to leave a creative mark. Something tangible that expresses artistically who and what I am as a human being. The purpose of my life is to leave my creative gift behind for others to enjoy.

Q: What are your priorities?

A: My children . . . I want them to understand who I am and why I choose the life I have. They're still young, but they're old enough to start grasping some of my values. Maybe they'll pursue their dreams and go against the grain if they feel the need and take a risk because I took the chance and tried to make it work.

Q: What do you do in your life that reflects your priorities?

A: I ignore the fears that keep cropping up in my head when I'm waking up in the morning and ignore what negative things people have to say. Being an artist is hard enough without trying to fit into someone else's idea of what being successful means. It's hard but not always a hopeless struggle, especially when I take the time for me to enjoy my moment of freedom and inner growth and not have to worry about doing it on someone else's time or schedule.

Favorite Book: Earth's Children series by Jean M. Auel
Favorite Web site: *www.historicstockade.com*
Favorite CD/Album: My current favorite: Avril Lavigne.
Favorite Quote: "A beaten path is for a beaten man."

"I had been feeling anxious about my life.
My children were growing up, my chosen career
of acting wasn't fruitful, and something inside
of me that I call my 'inner wisdom' created
such a sense of anxiety that I had
to pay attention to it."

—Judith Fraser, MFT
Psychotherapist, actress, writer

Q: *Was there a moment when you realized that you weren't on the right path, and that you needed to get on the right path regardless of the short-term consequences?*

A: I had been feeling anxious about my life. My children were growing up, my chosen career of acting wasn't fruitful and something inside of me that I call my "inner wisdom" created such a sense of anxiety that I had to pay attention to it. I went to see a psychologist, and while working with him I knew that I could do what he was doing.

It hit me like a bolt of lightning. The consequences were that I had to change my life. I had to let go of working in theater, being overly available to my husband and children (to say nothing about being available to every neighborhood child who needed a surrogate parent) and focus on me. I had been overindulging my family to avoid figuring out what I wanted to do with my life.

The path has given me much more than I ever imagined possible. My work is a shared journey with each of the clients who need education, inspiration and guidance so they too can reach out to find their own individual life-enhancing and spiritual ways.

Pain is always a great motivator for me. My body signals me through stress that I need to become aware of something beyond my present way of thinking or acting.

Q: *What do you do differently now in your life that reflects your priorities?*

A: I'm more aware of my judgments so that I can learn from them and let them go. I'm less needy about others meeting my expectations. I'm pretty much myself wherever I am.

Q: *What difficulties (if any) are there in living a more authentic life without retreating from the world entirely?*

A: I need more time alone. I feel different. I don't connect to as many people as I used to. I don't take care of others, I assist them in becoming more aware of how to take care of themselves. I listen rather than do.

Q: *Do you feel misunderstood?*

A: Not by my family and friends. I think they all respect who I am just as I respect who they are.

Q: *Do you care what others think?*

A: If someone has misinterpreted my actions as being negative towards them in some way, I care enough to let them know what my intentions were and clear up the misunderstanding as best as I can. Then I let go of their judgment. I care what others think and

I'm interested in their views, even if they're different than mine. I should say I'm interested in their views if they leave space for me to have different views as well. So, if what they think and say helps me, I care, if it doesn't help me then I let it go.

Q: *Do you hope to meet others who share your values?*

A: It just happens. I don't have to work at it.

Q: *What are your priorities and how do they affect your life now?*

A: My priority is to feel peaceful inside myself most of the time. And when I'm not peaceful, to figure out why and take action if I can to recreate that peace.

Favorite Book: *Dictionary of Symbols and Imagery* by Ad de Vries
Favorite Web site: *www.askjeeves.com*
Favorite CD/Album: *Gregorian Chants*
Favorite Quote: "Every problem is a gift." —Richard Bach

CHAPTER TEN

Typical Questions (and Some Answers)

Q. Where Do I Start to Transition into a More Meaningful Career?

First, I'll tell you where *not* to start. The worst place to start is by worrying about how you'll make money. If you only work for a paycheck, the odds are against you finding something that will satisfy your desire to do something interesting, helpful or meaningful. (On the other hand, if you *never* find a way to get paid for what you do, it will be a hobby and not a career.)

The second worst place to start is to simply find something you're *good* at. Women are especially prone to this mistake. If someone tells us we're good at something, and that they couldn't do it without us, we suddenly forget that we have our *own* criteria that determines what *we* find interesting or meaningful.

That said, the best place to start is by exploring what you're attracted to. If you already have some ideas about that, flesh out those ideas. Slowly work toward including what you're good at. Then investigate what you can get paid for. But in that order!

What if I Don't Know What I'm Attracted To? Can I Start With the Second Step?

No, don't skip to determining what you're good at until you know what you're drawn to. Stick with this until you have some definite starting points for career opportunities.

If you have no idea what you're drawn toward, then start trying to uncover your deep interests.

Exercise: Carry a small notebook with you to record topics and issues that capture your imagination. Pay attention when you're listening to the news and talk shows, and when you're browsing in a bookstore, library, or magazine rack. What headlines make you read further? Why? What topics are you passionate about?

Trail Marker: *The fastest answers are the most superficial answers. Don't rush just so you'll have something concrete to reduce your anxiety of the unknown. If you can allow yourself to be in limbo for a little while, you'll discover much more valuable answers than you will if you need to wrap up your search right away.*

For more on this topic:

Chapter 1: Read about listening to your calling.

Chapter 6: Read about using a Mission Statement to get and stay focused.

Q. What if I Can't Afford to Work Less in Order to Spend More Time on Personal and Family Goals?

You're probably torn between not being able to *financially* afford to work less, and not being able to *physically*, *emotionally* and *spiritually* afford to continue living as you are right now— spending too little time on what you care about most. This is a frustrating and scary place to be.

Assuming that you can't give notice at your full-time job tomorrow, what can you do to free up your time, your mind and your spirit so you can pay more attention to your family, your long-term goals and to taking care of yourself? One problem many of us have with making big changes is that we're either in denial that we need to change, or we suddenly realize that we're not on track and we want to change everything right away. Neither extreme is very productive.

1. Contemplate your priorities.

If you're a parent, think about what you need to do to meet your children's basic developmental needs. Seek out objective information about this. You can study child development or consult with an expert in early childhood development and attachment theory who can help you understand what your children need from you. Don't assume you're doing everything wrong, or that you're doing it all right. First learn more and then decide what's needed.

If you don't have pressing family concerns and you have the freedom to explore your personal growth as your top priority, ask yourself:

- What are you aspiring toward?

- What gets in the way of your being more fulfilled?
- How can you better understand your purpose in life and how can you spend your time and energy on what matters most?

2. Plan for the long-term:

Once you have some ideas about your direction, you can plan your long-term strategy to get there. Plan how you'll reduce your working hours outside the home and increase the amount of time spent on your personal growth and family time. This may take several months or even longer, depending on your specific situation and how tangled it's become. Identify other resources to help you find a little time here and there for yourself. For example, if you don't have extended family nearby to help with occasional, brief baby-sitting, can you swap baby-sitting with a trusted friend?

3. Short-term planning:

Now that you understand what your child needs, or what your priorities are for your personal growth and family, you're ready for a short-term plan. Your short-term plan includes how to take care of your immediate needs and problems, like paying the bills. But it also includes steps toward your long-term plan. It's critical to fit steps toward your *long-term plan* into your *day-to-day life*.

4. Revise your plans as you act on them:

The last piece of the puzzle is to re-evaluate and revise your short- and long-term plans as you go. Your circumstances, and your understanding of your needs and your situation, will change as you work your plans. As you work toward your long-term goals, you'll realize that not only is it possible to get there, but that nothing short of achieving your goals is worthwhile. Once you get out of survival mode and start noticing how much your family enjoys and benefits from your being relaxed and fun to be with, not being fully present with them will no longer feel like an option. You'll be motivated to find a way to make the necessary changes.

For more on this topic:

Chapter 6: Read about how to use both short-term and long-term plans to bring your most important goals into each day.

Chapter 7: Read about how hidden conflicts undermine your most cherished goals, and how to resolve them.

Q. How Do I Get My Partner's Support to Make These Changes?

Depending on why you're in this relationship, there are different reasons why your partner may not be supportive.

- You might be with someone who supports the wrong part of you.
- You might be asking the impossible from a basically supportive partner.

1) **Are you with someone who supports the wrong part of you?**

Many women get into relationships with men because they feel unsure of themselves and want someone to boost them up. There are lots of books on this topic, but the condensed version of this problem is that when he boosts you up, he's probably boosting the wrong part of you. And the flip side of finding someone to boost you up when you don't feel adequate is that there's a part of you that may want him to agree with you that you are inadequate. So you may not even be getting a boost after all.

You can only change this type of relationship by changing how you feel about yourself. The more you can face your inadequacies and stop needing anyone else to fill them in, the more of a whole person you will be. A good man will welcome this, and support you being whole. An insecure man will be threatened by this, and will try what he can to keep you feeling off balance.

Anytime you change a relationship, expect some resistance to that change. But use your judgment to decide if your partner is simply trying to figure out what's going on in your new behavior, or if he liked being with you better when you were insecure and needed him to boost you up.

2) Are you asking the impossible of a basically supportive partner?

This is a very common problem among women I work with. They want their partner to be interested in, and even excited about, every detail of their day, every sliver of an idea about their career and worst of all, their every mood shift!

This is not what your partner is there for. Thank God that men are (ideally) less likely to rush off on a burst of energy or be crushed when their latest idea wasn't the answer to all of life's questions. We need to be around someone stable and should be thankful that they aren't swept up with our every mood. Do you really want someone to remember every idea you've ever had and keep bringing it up long after you realized that it wasn't right for you? Then, you need to respect the fact that your partner doesn't want to hear about your every thought.

On the other hand, if you have a partner who doesn't support your overall growth and maturity, but wants you to stay insecure, unfulfilled or otherwise miserable because they feel better about themselves when you're unhappy, you've picked the wrong guy. Try to be objective when you talk about this with him and do your best to show that you're trying to become a deeper, more grounded and mature woman. Listen to what he has to say. If you're going about your changes in a way that is inconsiderate of him, or if you're ignoring some important family responsibilities, then you have to find a way to work on your growth while still taking care of your most important responsibilities and priorities.

For more on this topic:

Chapter 8: Read "How Supportive is Your Support System" and use the Support Systems worksheet.

Q. How Can I Make Time for Myself When Every Minute Is Spent Either on My Work or with My Family?

If you have a family that needs a tremendous amount of your time and energy, this is a tough dilemma. For example, if you have an infant, one or more children under the age of six, or a disabled child or spouse, your family does need an incredible amount of your time and energy. Most bright, resourceful women have already tried various ways to balance their lives. If you're still not able to find any time for yourself, it's either because you have more to do than you can handle, or because there are blind spots that are preventing you from carving out a few hours a week that you can spend any way you like.

Is Your Life Too Full?

If because of life circumstances, you simply have too much to do in too little time, there's less you can do to get relief. Make sure you've tried some obvious ways to get a little more time back:

- Swap baby-sitting with another adult you trust if that is feasible.
- Examine your lifestyle for extras that you can live without if that will cut back your expenses and therefore your hours spent working to pay for them.
- Determine how you can prevent adding to your burden. If part of your problem is that you volunteer for too many activities, or that you are trying to start up a company with twin newborns, then you must refocus on your priorities and stop doing work that is taking you away from them. You can start another company someday, but you can't redo your infants' earliest years later. And volunteering is great, but don't choose helping someone else when your own family needs you, or when you give up the personal time that you need for your own growth and refueling.

What You Can't See Can Hurt You

If you have some blind spots that are getting in the way, psychotherapy and/or coaching with someone who can help you gain some insight into your blind spots can be effective. If you schedule nonstop structured activities for your children, that's not good for them, and it's robbing you of valuable time and energy. If you're unfocused and give away your time based on guilt, a need for others (or your own need) to think you can do it all, that's unproductive and isn't fair to you or your family. If you're a workaholic (in other words, you work compulsively, not just to get a job done), you may have a hard time delegating and letting go of tasks that you don't need to do yourself. You may be very conflicted between wanting to have a life, and feeling anxious when you have unstructured time that isn't filled with work-related duties.

And if you're burning out or depressed, you may feel exhausted and unable to use the time you have. This can feel like never having enough time, and you certainly won't have much energy, either. Please see a reputable psychiatrist or psychotherapist if you think you might be depressed or burned out. This is treatable with the right professional help. At least consult with a professional so you can make better decisions about what to do.

But for those of you who are keeping yourselves too busy, or just have so many important responsibilities that there is very little quality time left over, please focus in on one top priority and make sure you're working toward that most important part of your life.

For more on this topic:

Chapter 1: Read about some of the myths we believe about work and free time.

Chapter 2: Read about how women who rely on adrenaline can get burned out and how to live in a more natural rhythm, or flow.

Chapter 5: Read about parenting burnout.

Chapter 6: Read about getting focused on what matters most.

Appendix A: Depression Self-Test: Read the symptoms of burnout and depression to see if you may need to get a professional evaluation and possibly treatment.

Q. I Know I Need to Get Help from Experts, but How Can I Prevent Being Vulnerable to Bad Advice?

This is a valid concern. Unfortunately there are many people offering advice who don't have wisdom. I can't think of a profession whose members don't include more causes for embarrassment than role models. My fields, coaching and psychotherapy, are definitely on that list. The good news is that you probably have an internal device, often called a B.S. detector, that will point you in the right direction most of the time.

1. *Do You Have a Reliable B.S. Detector?*

Are you rarely surprised when someone you know well divulges a dark secret? Is it fairly easy for you to decide with whom to share personal information, and with whom to be simply polite? When you read a well-written mystery, are you onto the bad guy in the first couple of chapters? Then you're probably going to make the right decision with coaches or therapists 99 percent of the time. Some people are talented sociopaths who can fool just about anyone. Don't worry too much about them, except to know that they exist. It's worse to be overly cynical than it is to get fooled by someone really crafty. If you have good judgment, you'll probably catch on to the bad guys before they do much harm just by using your common sense.

2. *What if Your B.S. Detector Isn't Reliable?*

If you're often surprised by people who seem nice but turn out not to be, you need to learn how to use your intuition and work on your judgment of others a little bit more.

Many women can be poor judges of character for several reasons:

1) We care too much about whether the other person likes us, and ignore their character flaws.

2) We want to be nice, and we think that means being nice to people who themselves aren't nice people.

3) The other person reminds us of someone we know and we assume they have qualities of that person. For example. we may think someone is a warm, caring person like our mom, so we trust they have our best interest in mind.

4) We're too trusting, or too cynical, of others, and we don't see them for who they really are. In other words, we might have an agenda that gets in the way of observing the other person objectively.

Strive for wanting to know the truth about yourself, and seek out professionals with wisdom, not just experience and degrees, who will tell you the truth. And trust your B.S. detector.

The Basics:
- Don't give anyone large sums of money up front, or pay for something you don't want or need.
- Don't give out your social security number unless you're going to a therapist, psychiatrist or physician, and they need it for insurance billing.
- Learn to tell the difference between what you don't want to hear, and the truth.
- No matter a coach's or therapist's qualifications, you need to feel a rapport with them for them to be helpful to you. An important part of the treatment is based on the relationship.
- If something doesn't feel right, it probably isn't, so wait a couple of days and see how you feel when you have some distance from the person.

APPENDIX A
DEPRESSION SELF-TEST

Are you wondering whether you're suffering from burnout or depression? Here is a checklist of symptoms of depression and burnout so you can get an idea of which you may be struggling with.[33] You may have symptoms of both burnout and depression.

If you check more than one or two boxes, you may need to see a mental health and/or medical professional.

Symptoms of Career Burnout

Do you:

❏ feel like you don't care about your job performance nearly as much as you used to?

❏ feel like you've been wasting your life on things that don't ultimately matter?

❏ feel exhausted or worn out?

❏ feel like your job is so routine that it's hard to care about it anymore?

❏ feel demoralized (for example, you've stopped trying to come up with solutions to problems at work because nothing ever changes)?

❏ watch the clock at work and feel a sense of relief when it's time to leave for the day?

---

[33] *This is not a complete list of symptoms of depression. See a mental health professional for more information, or to make a diagnosis and prescribe treatment.*

Symptoms of Parenting Burnout

Do you:

❑ feel like you're on overload, and don't have much patience with your children?

❑ feel more like a maid, cook, chauffeur than a valuable part of your child's life?

❑ feel unappreciated?

❑ feel like as soon as you get through the day, it's time to go to sleep and start all over again?

Symptoms of Depression

Do you:

❑ feel a loss of interest in activities you usually enjoy?

❑ feel sad, down or hopeless?

❑ feel guilty, worthless or useless?

❑ feel extremely tired, to the point where others have noticed how fatigued you are?

❑ have a significant increase or decrease in weight?

❑ have a very hard time concentrating and remembering things?

❑ have a hard time falling asleep or staying asleep? Or are you sleeping too much?

APPENDIX B
CHAPTER RESOURCES[34]

Chapter 1 Resources
Books

Entrepreneur of Life: Faith and the Venture of Purposeful Living (*The Trinity Forum Study Series*) (Edited by: OS Guinness, Ginger Koloszyc and Karen Lee-Thorp)—Every person has a unique calling to count for good. An entrepreneur of life is one who responds to this call—who takes it on as a creative challenge, a venture of faith for the sake of good.

The Five Stages of the Soul (Harry Moody, Ph.D.): An enjoyable book full of anecdotes of seekers, mythological tales and a map for the development of the soul.

Get Clark Smart: The Ultimate Guide to Getting Rich From America's Money-Saving Expert—I'm a huge fan of Clark Howard, consumer advocate, radio talk show host, author and all-around great guy. Clark made enough money from selling a chain of travel agencies in 1987 to retire at age 31. Instead, he's made it his mission to help consumers avoid getting ripped off and to keep more of what they earn. His Web site has great resources, tips and links—*www.clarkhoward.com*. His other book is *Clark's Big Book of Bargains*.

Living the Simple Life (Elaine St. James)—My personal favorite of the books on simplifying your life to create more time and energy to devote to what is really important. (Other books by Elaine St. James: *Simplify Your Work Life*, *Simplify Your Life With Kids*, and *Inner Simplicity*.)

Stopping: How to Be Still When You Have to Keep Going (Dr. David Kundtz)— Another book on how to create time and space in your life.

Take Your Time: Finding Balance in a Hurried World (Eknath Easwaran)—A wonderful little book that makes taking your time seem so completely obvious, you'll wonder why you didn't think of it yourself.

---

[34] *I repeat sources when they appear in more than one chapter to make it easier for readers who don't read each chapter to find the resources they're looking for.*

Talking Zen (Alan Watts)—While this book contains some interesting ideas and well-written sections, I would recommend other books by Alan Watts, especially to those who aren't familiar with him. His books are mostly compiled lectures, some edited posthumously by his son. Some titles I would recommend include: *The Book: On the Taboo Against Knowing Who You Are, The Wisdom of Insecurity,* and *This is It, and Other Essays on Zen and Spiritual Experience.* I also recommend audio tapes by Watts. He had a wonderful speaking voice, a charming English accent, and was a master lecturer.

Voluntary Simplicity: Toward a Way of Life That is Outwardly Simple, Inwardly Rich (Duane Elgin)—The pioneering book on the subject, and still pertinent.

Web Sites

www.lowermybills.com—This site lets you easily compare rates and benefits on a variety of services like health and auto insurance, cell phone service, and credit cards. Lowering your debt is an important step toward living a more simple life, and this site and others like it can help.

Simple Living Magazine—*www.simpleliving.com* You can also get the magazine on most newsstands.

People Quoted

Julia Wilkinson, author of *Best Bang for Your Book, My Life at AOL* and *What Sells on eBay for What*
Web site: *http://www.aolmemorabilia.com/clkbnksales.html*
E-mail: *juliawilk@aol.com*

Elaine Allison, owner of Canine's Best Behavior
Phone: 323-255-1522
Web site: *http://caninesbestbehavior.com*
E-mail: *dedawgbrawd@aol.com*

Chapter 2 Resources
Books

Finding Flow: The Psychology of Engagement with Everyday Life (Mihaly Csikszentmihalyi)—This is a useful book to learn more about how he defines and understands "flow."

Hare Brain, Tortoise Mind: How Intelligence Increases When You Think Less (Guy Claxton)—Claxton's book makes the case that the slower, intuitive mind is actually more effective than the fast "hare brain" logical mind we're used to relying on for decision making.

Reflections on the Art of Living: A Joseph Campbell Companion, (Edited by Diane K. Osbon)—This book is compiled from a series of lectures. His most famous book about the "Hero's Journey," which is found in many cultures, *The Hero With a Thousand Faces*, is also worth reading.

The Seeking Self: The Quest for Self-Improvement and the Creation of Personal Suffering (Richard Lind, Ph.D.)—Lind discusses the harmful side of constantly seeking. Specifically, even when we're seeking something "positive," we're aspiring for an ideal that is always out of reach, and we're setting ourselves up to never be satisfied.

Tao Te Ching (Lao Tzu)—This classic book was said to be written on the spot by the ancient master, Lao Tzu. He was leaving town, and someone asked him to explain how to live properly. So he wrote down a few tips . . . and 2,500 years later, they're still relevant. Like any timeless wisdom, he didn't tell what happened, but what always happens. (There are many translations, some better than others. I like the Mitchell translation.)

Chapter 3 Resources
Books

Diamond Heart Series (A.H. Almaas)—Almaas' books in this series are from his lectures. He offers a great deal of help understanding who we are in our "Essence" and how to disidentify with our "Ego." I especially like *Indestructible Innocence*, Number 4 in the series, and *Elements of the Real in Man*, Number 1 in the series.

Reflections on the Art of Living: A Joseph Campbell Companion, (Edited by Diane K. Osbon)—This book is compiled from a series of lectures. His most famous book about the "Hero's Journey," which is found in many cultures, *The Hero With a Thousand Faces*, is also worth reading.

Web Site

VH1's *Behind the Music*—*www.vh1.com*. Go to VH1 *shows*, then to *Behind the Music*.

Chapter 4 Resources

Books

Creating a Life Worth Living: A Practical Course in Career Design for Artists, Innovators, and Others Aspiring to a Creative Life (Carol Lloyd)—An excellent book to help discover the right day job, as well as how to navigate the rough waters of having a creative career and life.

Management Books:
Even if you're not an entrepreneur or a manager, you may want to understand what your boss should be doing. These books can help you understand your company's flaws and strengths.

The Art of Waking People Up (Kenneth Cloke and Joan Goldsmith)—Joan and coauthor and husband Kenneth, whom I admire greatly, continue to teach others to bring out the best in employees and to be visionary leaders.

Built to Last: Successful Habits of Visionary Companies (James Collins and Jerry Porras)—Real-life examples of role-model companies, this book also studies long-range success of such companies.

Deming Management at Work (Mary Walton)—This book and Dr. Deming's work are geared toward large manufacturing plants. However, any size business can benefit from Dr. Deming's Total Quality Management principles. Not a trend, TQM is a great model for today's businesses.

The Effective Executive (Peter Drucker)—Drucker wrote a lot of books. It's hard to pick one to recommend, but this one is practical and easy to read.

Why Leaders Can't Lead (Warren Bennis)—Bennis is not afraid to tell the truth. His points are well taken and include helpful ideas about how to improve your leadership ability and skills.

Web Sites

www.Entreworld.org (remember, it's .org)—The whole site is great, but also check out the "FastTrac" section. The link is in the lower left hand corner.

www.Fabjob.com—In addition to their publication on how to find a "fab job," this site also has articles on lots of topics, including how to transition out of your career into something you'll enjoy better or find more satisfying. Go to the "fabadvice" page for these articles and tips.

www.Inc.com—A useful magazine, but an even better Web site. There are lots of interesting articles and resources online. It's mostly for entrepreneurs, but they do have quite a few articles on management, trends and other topics.

http://peerspectives.org—Edward Lowe Peerspectives. Great resource for business owners, including helpful articles and tips.

http://www.score.org—The Service Corps of Retired Professionals is a free service offered by the Small Business Administration. You can ask questions by e-mail, find out about their network of volunteer business consultants and link to the Patent and Trademark Office as well as the Electronic Resource Commerce Center.

http://www.sba.gov—Small Business Administration. The SBA Web site has some good articles, legal information and a list of frequently researched topics. There is a section on women-owned businesses, as well.

Chapter 5 Resources

Parenting Books

Discover Your Child's Learning Style: Children Learn in Unique Ways—Here's the Key to Every Child's Learning Success (Willis and Hodson)—Helps you identify your child's (or your) learning style so you can work with their natural abilities, not against them. There's a profile test in the book. Or get a discount online if you use the code FiredUp100 when you purchase the profile online (*www.learningsuccesscoach.com*).

The Fussy Baby (William Sears, M.D.)—Many parents don't have easy babies, and it's not because they're inadequate parents. Some babies are fussy by nature, and this book helps you identify if your baby is a fussy baby and what to do about it. This could make a real impact on your quality of life and parenting if you have a fussy baby.

The High-Need Baby (William Sears, M.D.)—Another wonderful book by the author of *The Fussy Baby* that helps parents who have premature, seriously ill, autistic babies or those with a birth defect of any kind that interferes with the parent-infant bonding process.

I Heard it Through the Playground (Fram, Boswell, & Maas)—Hundreds of tips and hints that would take years of playground time to hear on your own.

More Energy Now! How to Beat Mommy Burnout and Live with Vitality, Passion, and Joy (Susie Michelle Cortright) This interesting book seems to be only available on Cortright's Web site: *http://www.momscape.com.*

Siblings Without Rivalry (Faber & Mazlish)—Practical advice about the normal day-to-to challenges of raising siblings. Each chapter has an easy to read summary to make it easy to review for specific tips.

Touchpoints (T. Berry Brazelton)—This book describes critical points in development, or "touchpoints," and babies' needs so parents can respond to them. Dr. Brazelton has a friendly tone without speaking down to his audience.

Your Baby & Child (Penelope Leach)—An expert on infants and children explains in a very straightforward way what your baby needs and why. The chapter on sleeping issues is especially helpful. I keep a copy of this book in my waiting room, and frequently recommend it to my clients.

Other Books Mentioned

A Guide for the Perplexed (E.F. Schumacher)—Answers a lot of "why" questions that science or reason alone can't. This is a small book, and very enjoyable to read. I found that it helped me to think more clearly about some important issues.

Happiness Is a Serious Problem: A Human Nature Repair Manual (Dennis Prager)— A primer on how to combat threats to our happiness written by someone who feels it is our moral responsibility to be happy. Prager also has a national radio show, and devotes the second hour of his show each Friday to the subject of happiness. *www.dennisprager.com*

Web Sites for Parents

www.family.go.com
A Disney site that offers activities and other fun stuff to do with your kids on days when your creativity needs a little inspiration.

iVillage.com has a great deal of information on everything from infertility to the empty nest syndrome. They sponsor chats, offer quizzes, and you can link to many magazine Web sites from their homepage. They don't always support being "inwardly mobile," but you can navigate to those articles that support your point of view.
iVillage also sponsors stand-alone sites like:
- Parent Soup: *www.parentsoup.com* This Web site has lots of information for parents of children of all ages.
- Parents Place: *www.parentsplace.com* More parenting information on a variety of topics.

MOMS Clubs —*www.momsclub.org*
Great resource for stay-at-home moms. There are groups that meet in every community for support, talks and play dates. And moms even get a night out every month at many clubs.

Autism Resources—*http://www.autism-resources.com/links.html*
This site contains resources divided into categories including sites with definitions of autism, news, accounts, treatments, bibliography and an entire separate category dedicated to Aspergers Syndrome. Click on Main Page at the top for other categories, including information for parents who have just found out that their child is autistic.

Experts Quoted

Margaret Carlisle Duncan, Professor of Human Movement Sciences at University of Wisconsin-Milwaukee and author of "Stories We Tell Ourselves about Ourselves," Sociology of Sport Journal, 1998, Volume 15, pp. 95-108.
Phone: 414-229-5341
E-mail: *mduncan@uwm.edu*

Mariaemma Pellulo Willis
www.learningsuccesscoach.com
This is the Web site for the book listed above on discovering your child's unique learning style. My readers can get a discount on the online profile. Just click on The Online Profile and use the following code for a $5 discount: FiredUp100

Joan Maltese, Ph.D.
Child Development Institute, Woodland Hills, CA
The Child Development Institute provides education, support and therapy to children and their parents, teachers and professionals who care for them.
Web site: *www.childdevelopmentinstitute.org*
Phone: 818-888-4559

Reverend Sandra Yarlott
Director, Department of Spiritual Care, UCLA Medical Center
Phone: (310) 825-7484
E-mail: *syarlott@mednet.ucla.edu*
Program webpage: *www.acpe.edu* (UCLA information is in the Pacific Region)

Resources for Working from Home

Working from home is, in many ways, like working anywhere. So some of the resources you might use for developing any business may be very useful if you want to work from home, like *businessknowhow.com*, *entreworld.org* and *myownbusiness.org*. You may even find a job opportunity on the employment search engines like *Monster.com* or your local newspaper's classified ad sites, and explore whether the employer is willing to have an employee work from home if you get an interview.

Important Note: *Please use your judgment with all work-at-home resources.*

At-Home Mothers—*www.athomemothers.com*
The site of The National Association of At-Home Mothers. They charge an $18 fee for membership, but also have free info guides available on the Web site. For example, they have a helpful article on making the business case for a flexible schedule on this page: *www.athomemothers.com/infoguides/36a6.htm*

Entrepreneurial Parent—*http://www.en-parent.com*

www.drlaura.com
Dr. Laura's site includes articles, book recommendations and other supportive information for stay-at-home moms as well as a whole section dedicated to helping moms make the transition to being a work-at-home mom.

Home-Based *Parents*—*www.home-based-parents.com*
Home-Based Parents offers moral and online business support for home-based business opportunities run by work-at-home moms on the Internet. They also have the APPP Ezine, a bi-weekly publication delivered via e-mail filled with family-friendly humor, business tips and marketing resources.

Home-Based Working Moms—*www.hbwm.com*
A professional association and online community of parents who work at home and those who would like to. HBWM members receive a monthly (print) newsletter, free advertising options, Hire-A-Mom directory listing, national publicity opportunities, email discussion list, private message boards, support, networking, work-at-home scam alerts and other helpful information.

Work at Home Careers—*www.workathomecareers.com*
Free work-at-home job searches, work from home job alerts, articles and work-at-home scam alerts.

Work-at-Home Moms site—*www.wahm.com*
An online magazine with links to job search engines, articles on working from home and other issues of interest to those who want to work from home.

Chapter 6 Resources
Books

Creating a Life Worth Living: A Practical Course in Career Design for Artists, Innovators, and Others Aspiring to a Creative Life (Carol Lloyd)—This book captures the useful and interesting process Ms. Lloyd has developed over many years in her workshops to help the reader do just what the title promises. *www.igc.org/lifeworthliving*

The Path (Laurie Beth Jones)—This book helps readers write their Mission Statement. It's written from a Christian point of view, but I think most people would find its concepts useful.

Seven Habits of Highly Effective People by (Steven Covey)—One of the first books to acknowledge family responsibilities when running a business or pursuing a career. This book can also help you with your Mission Statement.

Soul Without Shame: A Guide to Liberating Yourself from the Judge Within (Byron Brown)—A guide to understanding our "inner critic" and useful tools to disarm it.

Other Resources

Gale Encyclopedia of Professional Organizations—most libraries have this directory.

Yahoo online directory of professional organizations:
http://dir.yahoo.com/business_and_economy/organizations/professional/

www.careervoyages.gov—Career Voyages is an effort by the Department of Labor and the Department of Education to link the educational community with the world of work. There are several interesting resources here. You can "Chart Your Course," choose an industry and see both the projected job growth for a variety of careers in that industry and see the median U.S. wage for that industry over several different education levels. You can also see what's hot; either overall or by state, jobs that don't require a four-year degree, or jobs that require a four-year degree or better.

www.businessknowhow.com

Janet Attard is the author of *Home Office and Small Business Answer Book* and *Business Know-How: An Operational Guide for Home-Based and Micro-Sized Businesses*. She is also the founder and CEO of *www.businessknow how.com*, an online resource for small-business owners and those thinking about starting their own business. The Web site offers a huge amount of articles on topics of interest to small business owners and also has an interactive message board where members (the membership is free) can post questions. Janet answers many of the questions, as do others on the boards.

People Who Volunteered Their Mission Statements

Elaine Allison: Canine's Best Behavior
Phone: 323-255-1522
Web site: *http://caninesbestbehavior.com*
E-mail: *dedawgbrawd@aol.com*

Shirley Oya: Money Coach
Phone: 818-893-8484
E-mail: *YMM4Coach@aol.com*

Mary Mora:Training Coordinator, JanS.T.A.R.
Phone: 336-775-9622
E-mail: *mgjanstar@yahoo.com*

Chapter 7 Resources

Books

Organized to Be the Best!: Simplify and Improve How You Work (Susan Silver)—Great tips on being organized, and more important, being productive. I also like that Susan cautions readers against becoming compulsively organized.

Meditation Books

How to Meditate (LaShan, McDonald, and Novak)—A guide for beginners.

Meditation (Eknath Easwaran)—Meant for novices, this book provides insight into applying meditation in everyday life.

Meditation for Dummies (Stephan Bodian)—I don't like the "Dummies" in the title, but this is a very helpful book on meditation and includes some history, explanation of what you can get from meditating and some great meditation exercises. I recommend this book often as a good starting point to meditation.

Relaxation Response (Benson)—A useful book on meditation that is non-spiritual and non-religious.

Expert Quoted

Wayne Lehrer's website—*http://www.prodigywithin.com*

Chapter 8 Resources

Can Love Last? (Stephen A. Mitchell)—Mitchell believes that love is key to a life worth living. He explains in this book how to keep love growing in long-term relationships, and what gets in the way. One point he makes is that love isn't an illusion. Rather, safety is an illusion. And he makes a convincing case that it takes courage to make love last.

The 7 Habits of Highly Effective People, First Things First (Steven Covey)—Covey gives lots of examples of how to stay in touch with what is most important to you while dealing with day-to-day business and family responsibilities.

Mapping the Terrain of the Heart: Passion, Tenderness, and the Capacity to Love (Stephen Goldbart, Ph.D. and David Wallin, Ph.D.)—The authors point out what may be getting in the way of maintaining a loving relationship.

Synergy Plan Worksheet: The Path Is the Goal completed by Shirley Oya: Money Coach, Phone: 818-893-8484, E-mail: *YMM4Coach@aol.com*

Mentoring Resources

Here are two Web sites that can help you get involved as a mentor. I have not used either of these programs, so please check them out if you wish to get involved:

http://nmp.mentoring.org/kaplan/top_getinvolved.html
The National Mentoring Partnership is an advocate for the expansion of mentoring and a resource for mentors and mentoring initiatives nationwide. They provide support, resources and guidance for people to mentor young people in their communities. Their Web site has lots of great information, and if you click on About Us you can find out how they can help you become a mentor.

http://www.reach4it.com
Reach4it is a free online service connecting both teens and adults with volunteer online mentors who have experience or career path to share. They strive to help teens:
 • make career and financial decisions
 • get a good education
 • explore entrepreneurship
 • find answers to their questions
 • deal with obstacles and challenges

In case your child(ren) is/are inspired to volunteer, here's a useful Web site for students that want to do service projects:

www.ysa.org

Mentoring Quote Contributors
Michelle Hazlewood:
http://www.universalwellness.us
Personal Success Guide for the 21st Century
Universal Wellness (Fit Bodies), Thousand Oaks, CA
E-mail: *michelle@universalwellness.us*
Phone: 805-375-2516

Laurie Dea Owyang:
Humanasaurus, human resources consultants in Los Angeles
E-mail: *laurie@market-basedsolutions.com*
Phone: 323-663-6100

Mariaemma Willis:
Ventura, CA
805-648-1739
E-mail: *m@learningsuccesscoach.com*
Web site: *www.learningsuccesscoach.com*
Coauthor (with Victoria Hansen) of *Discover Your Child's Learning Style: Children Learn in Unique Ways—Here's the Key to Every Child's Learning Success.*

My readers can get a discount on the online profile. Just click on The Online Profile and use the following code for a $5 discount: FiredUp100

Chapter 9 Resources

Books

God in Search of Man: A Philosophy of Judaism (Abraham Joshua Heschel)— Heschel asserts that religion is not a vehicle by which humanity draws closer to God; it is always God who reaches out to humanity through religion. This book is one of Heschel's most popular books, but all of his books are well-written, scholarly and inspired.

Inner Christianity: A Guide to the Esoteric Tradition (Richard Smoley)—A very interesting basic guide to mystical or esoteric Christianity, which has a great deal in common with the esoteric aspects of all great religions.

Letters of a Scattered Brotherhood (Mary Strong)—A collection of anonymous letters by people on the spiritual path. The letters were written around the time of World War II.

Sri Aurobindo or the Adventure of Consciousness (Satprem)—Written by a devotee of Sri Aurobindo, a spiritual teacher and philosopher of the 20th Century, this book is an introduction to some of Sri Aurobindo's work and ideas. I have also found the question and answer format of *Letters on Yoga, Volumes I, II,* and *III* especially useful for understanding his philosophy and teachings.

Experts Quoted

Rev. Sandra Yarlott, Director
Department of Spiritual Care
UCLA Medical Center
10833 LeConte Avenue—17-348 CHS
Los Angeles, CA 90095-1733
Phone: (310) 825-7484
E-mail: *syarlott@mednet.ucla.edu*
Program Web page: *www.acpe.edu* (UCLA information is in the Pacific Region)

Interviews with the Inwardly Mobile

Margot Lester, Owner of The Word Factory
Writer and Consultant, covering business, love, sex, relationships and pop culture
for a variety of media, and author of two books: *The Real Life Guide to Life After
College*, and *The Real Life Guide to Starting Your Career*
Phone: 919-967-3477
Web site: *www.margotlester.com*
E-mail: *margotlester@earthlink.net*

David Allen, Owner, The David Allen Company
The David Allen Company is a professional training, coaching and management
consulting organization. David is the bestselling author of *Getting Things Done:
The Art of Stress-Free Productivity*. His new book is *Ready for Anything: 52
Productivity Principles for Work & Life*.
Phone: 805-646-8432
Web site: *www.davidco.com*
E-mail: *info@davidco.com*

Diana Moore, Realtor
Thousand Oaks, CA
Phone: 805-917-4117
Web site: *www.DianaMoore.com*
E-mail: *info@dianamoore.com*

Robert Laper
Artist, Antique Dealer, Art and Antique Restoration
Schenectady, NewYork (Stockade section)

Judith Fraser, MFT
Judith Fraser is a psychotherapist, actress and writer in Los Angeles, CA.
Phone: 323-656-9800
E-mail: *jfrasermft@speakeasy.net*

ABOUT THE AUTHOR

Leslie Godwin was born in Forest Hills, New York. She's been a psychotherapist for twenty years, and an entrepreneur for the last ten years, creating a type of Career & Life-Transition Coaching that helps people put their families, faith and principles first when making career and life choices. She's in private practice in Calabasas, California, as both a psychotherapist and coach.

Leslie has been a resource for *The Wall Street Journal*, *Business week.com*, *Fortune*, *USAToday.com*, CNN, Lifetime television network, *Los Angeles Times*, *Los Angeles Daily News*, *www.drlaura.com*, and other print and online media.

Leslie lives in Calabasas, California, with her husband, Bob, and their two Great Danes, Finn and Savannah.

Contact Leslie: *www.lesliegodwin.com*
Phone: (818) 880-4486
E-mail: *lesliegodwin@earthlink.net*